RHODE ISLAND

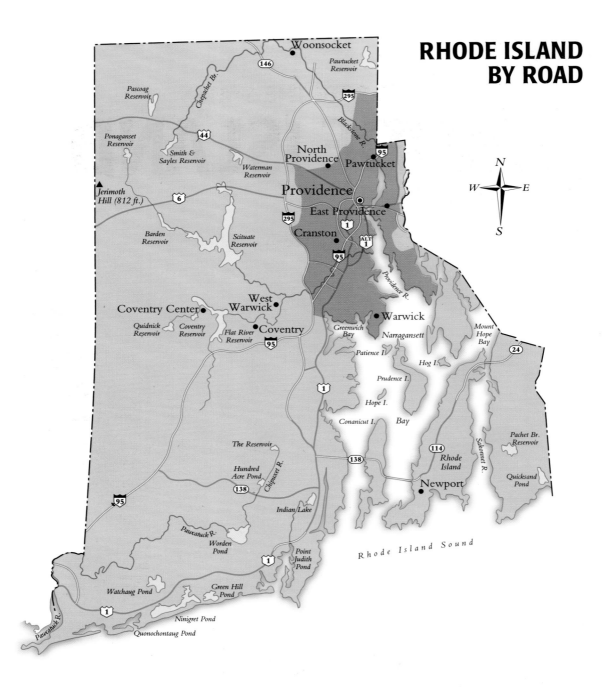

RHODE ISLAND
BY ROAD

Woonsocket

Pawtucket
Reservoir

146

Pascoag
Reservoir

Chepachet Br.

295

Blackstone R.

Ponaganset
Reservoir

44

Smith &
Sayles Reservoir

North
Providence

95

Pawtucket

*Waterman
Reservoir*

Providence

▲ Jerimoth
Hill (812 ft.)

6

East Providence

Barden
Reservoir

Scituate
Reservoir

295

Cranston

1

ALT
1

95

Providence R.

West
Warwick

Coventry Center

Warwick

Quidnick
Reservoir

Coventry
Reservoir

Flat River
Reservoir

Coventry

95

Greenwich
Bay

Narragansett

Mount
Hope
Bay

Patience I.

Hog I.

24

Chipuxet R.

1

Prudence I.

Hope I.

The Reservoir

Conanicut I.

Bay

*Pachet Br.
Reservoir*

Hundred
Acre Pond

138

114

Rhode
Island

Sakonnet R.

Quicksand
Pond

138

Indian Lake

Newport

Pawcatuck R.

Worden
Pond

1

Point
Judith
Pond

Rhode   Island   Sound

Watchaug Pond

Green Hill
Pond

1

Pawcatuck R.

Ninigret Pond

Quonochontaug Pond

Block Island

N
W   E
S

URBAN AREA

0   2   4   6   8   10   12
MILES

CELEBRATE THE STATES
RHODE ISLAND

Ted Klein

BENCHMARK BOOKS

MARSHALL CAVENDISH
NEW YORK

Benchmark Books
Marshall Cavendish Corporation
99 White Plains Road
Tarrytown, New York 10591-9001

Library of Congress Cataloging-in-Publication Data
Klein, Ted.
Rhode Island / by Ted Klein.
p.   cm. —— (Celebrate the states)
Includes bibliographical references and index.
Summary: An introduction to the geography, history, government,
economy, people, achievements, and landmarks of the country's
smallest state which is known as the Ocean State.
ISBN 0-7614-0417-1 (lib. bdg.)
1. Rhode Island—Juvenile literature. [1. Rhode Island.] I. Title. II. Series.
F79.3.K58   1999   974.5—dc21   97-47727   CIP   AC

Maps and graphics supplied by Oxford Cartographers, Oxford, England

Photo research by Ellen B. Dudley and Matthew J. Dudley

Cover photo: Paul Rezendes

The photographs in this book are used by permission and through the courtesy of: *All Rights Reserved the Historical Society of Rhode Island*: The Banishment of Roger Williams/c.1850/oil on canvas/Peter Frederick Rothermel/RHi(x5)20,32; Philip alias Metacomet of Pokanoket/1834 /Engraving/from the original as published by Church/RHi(x3)771, 36; Moses Brown/Engraving/ J.A.J. Wilcox/RHi(x3)2765,39(top); To be sold by John Miller at his house or store: a number of healthy negro boys/July 6, 1764/ink on paper/Providence Gazette and Country Journal/RHi(x3)5421,39(bottom); The Burning of The Gaspee, 1792/1892/oil on canvas/Charles DeWolf Brownell/RHi(x5)10,40; Pawtucket Bridge and Falls/c. 1812/ watercolor and ink on paper/D.B./RHi(x5)22,44; Sarah Helen Whitman/Albumen Print/Colemen Remington Photographic Studio/RHi(x3)3055,87(left); Edgar Allen Poe/Albumen Print/RHi(x3)605,87(right); Oliver Hazard Perry/Engraving/J.B. Forrest/RHi(x42)71, 95; Miss Annie S. Peck/Color Lithograph/RHi (x4)135,96; Nicholas Brown/1822/Engraving/H. Wright Smith/RHi(x3)4004,129; Julia Ward Howe/Albumen Print/RHi(x3)5978,130; Horace Mann/1884/Engraving/J. Sartain/RHi(x3)632, 132; Samuel Slater 1900/Engraving/J.W. Steel/RHi(x3)3049,133. *Redwood Library and Athenium, Newport, Gift of the Artist, 1859*: 28-29. *Slater Mill Historic Site*: 48. *Leslie M. Newman*: 58, 71,84- 85. *Brown University Library*: 89. © *Constance Brown*: 92(left). © *Jan Bindas Studios*: 92(right). © *Patrick O'Connor*: 94. Corbis-Bettmann: 31, 90. *UPI/Corbis-Bettmann*: 128. *Archive Photos*: Frank Capri/SAGA, 99; New York Times Co., 98; Christopher Felver, 131. © *Susan Cole Kelly*: 126. *Photo Researchers, Inc.*: Eunice Harris, 50-51, 125; Michael G. Gadomski, 119(top); Leonard Lee Rue, 119(bottom). Noble Proctor, 122(right); John Mitchell, 122(left). *Positive Images*: David Pratt, 10-11; Les Campbell, 18; Ivan Massar, 20; Patricia J. Bruno, 59; Jerry Howard, 62, 135; Candace Cochrane, 117. *The Image Bank*: Brett Froomer, 6-7; Steve Dunwell, 16, 23, 64, 103; Eric Schweikardt, 21; D. Van Kirk, 81; Eddie Hironaka, 108; Ira Block, 110, 112. *Paul Rezendes*: 13, 17, 26, 66, 109, 114, 116, back cover. *The National Audubon Society Collection/Photo Researchers, Inc.*: Jeff Lepore, 19. *David O'Connor*: 24, 68-69, 73, 76. *Ron Manville*: 60, 60(inset), 79. *Eliot Cohen*: 80, 100-101. *Sun Photo by Daniel Hyland*: 83.

Printed in Italy

3   5   6   4   2

CONTENTS

RHODE ISLAND IS . . .

1 A LITTLE UNIVERSE

Every state thinks of itself as special. Rhode Island *knows* that it is. Its most obvious distinction is geographic: it is the smallest of the fifty states. The next largest state, Delaware, is nearly twice as big. Rhode Island is only forty-eight miles long and thirty-seven miles wide; you could bicycle across it in a day. Though its official nickname is the Ocean State, it is affectionately called Little Rhody.

CARVED BY GLACIERS

Take a look at a map. You'll see that Rhode Island's shape resembles an upright rectangle pierced from below by the thin wedge of Narragansett Bay, splintering off the eastern portion of the state. Providence, Rhode Island's biggest city, sits at the top of the bay.

The narrow portion of the state on the eastern side of the bay seems like it should be part of Massachusetts rather than Rhode Island. If you study the map, you'll see that even though the town of Tiverton is connected by land to Massachusetts, you can't reach it from the main part of Rhode Island without taking a bridge.

The bay itself, penetrating twenty-eight miles into the state, is filled with three large islands and dozens of smaller ones, some no more than rocky outcroppings. The largest island, Aquidneck, contains the city of Newport. Another body of land, Block Island, lies twelve miles out at sea.

Although Rhode Island is never more than 48 miles wide, it boasts 400 miles of coastline, much of it on Narragansett Bay, easily earning its nickname "the Ocean State."

The coast's ragged look, like the rest of New England's geography, is largely the result of glaciers. About 100,000 years ago, the earth's climate cooled slightly and the polar ice cap began to spread south. As the ice advanced, it picked up rocks and stones. Using these the way a carpenter uses sandpaper, it carved out channels that became rivers and bays, and scoured out depressions that later became plains and lakes. Massive chunks of ice were left melting after the

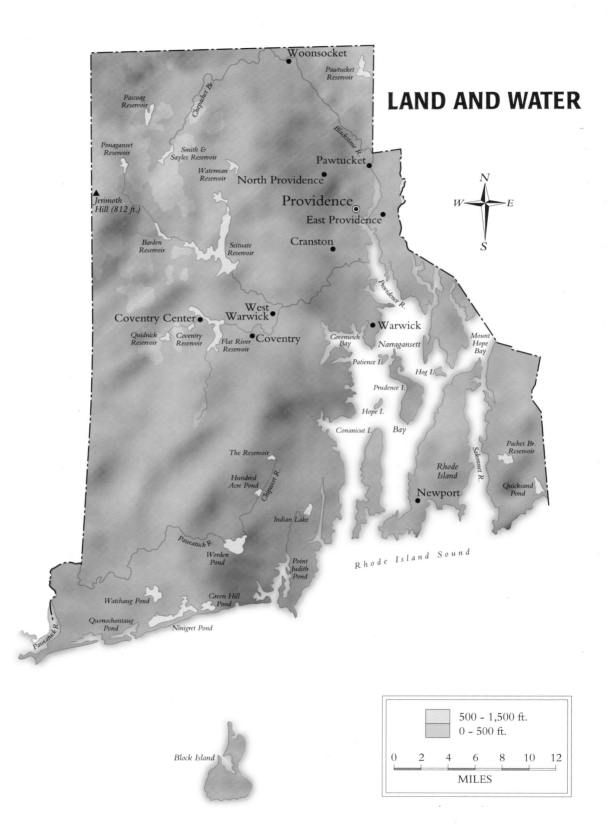

LAND AND WATER

Woonsocket

Pawtucket
Reservoir

Pascoag
Reservoir

Chepachet Br.

Blackstone R.

Ponaganset
Reservoir

Smith &
Sayles Reservoir

Waterman
Reservoir

Pawtucket

North Providence

Providence

▲ Jerimoth
Hill (812 ft.)

East Providence

Barden
Reservoir

Scituate
Reservoir

Cranston

Providence R.

West
Warwick

Coventry Center

Warwick

Quidnick
Reservoir

Coventry
Reservoir

Flat River
Reservoir

Coventry

Greenwich
Bay

Narragansett

Mount
Hope
Bay

Patience I.

Hog I.

Prudence I.

Pachet Br.
Reservoir

The Reservoir

Hope I.

Sakonnet R.

Hundred
Acre Pond

Chipuxet R.

Conanicut I.

Bay

Rhode
Island

Quicksand
Pond

Indian Lake

Newport

Pawcatuck R.

Worden
Pond

Point
Judith
Pond

Rhode Island Sound

Watchaug Pond

Green Hill
Pond

Quonochontaug
Pond

Pawcatuck R.

Ninigret Pond

N
W · E
S

	500 – 1,500 ft.
	0 – 500 ft.

Block Island

0   2   4   6   8   10   12
MILES

glaciers had retreated northward, forming freshwater ponds. Where the rock was strongest and most resistant, such as in the western part of the state, hills were left; where the rock was softest, as in the area east of Narragansett Bay, the land was flattened.

Even at their highest, the hills of Rhode Island are nothing to brag about. The state's highest point, Jerimoth Hill in Foster, near the Connecticut border, rises just 812 feet. You won't find much downhill skiing or mountain climbing in the Ocean State.

A LAND OF FORESTS

A 1930 travel guide boasted, "The amazing thing about this state is the diversity of its scenery, combining within its borders the lure of the sea and the beauty of the rolling hills." That's still true today. For so small a state, Rhode Island possesses an impressively varied landscape, from the hills in the north and west, to the flat coastal plains east of the bay, to the marshes, beaches, and tidal ponds along the southern shore.

In 1524, when the explorer Giovanni da Verrazano first ventured through Rhode Island, he described the woods as "so great and thicke" that an army could have hidden in them. In fact, the state is more wooded today than it was in the nineteenth century, when more land was devoted to farming. More than half of Rhode Island is once again covered with forests of oak, maple, pine, hickory, and other trees. You can walk today in woods that look as if they've been wild forever, only to discover ancient stone walls marking the boundaries of what was farmland in the eighteenth and nineteenth centuries.

Ancient giant oak trees still grace the Rhode Island landscape.

Throughout Rhode Island, old rock walls show where property lines once were.

"We have a lot of diversity, with both hardwood and softwood forests," says Brian Tefft, a state wildlife biologist. "What I myself like is to walk through a white pine forest . . . the breeze blowing through the pine needles sounds really beautiful."

Rhode Island's forests no longer teem with large wildlife, but occasionally a black bear or a moose wanders in from neighboring Massachusetts or Connecticut. There is a growing population of white-tailed deer, as well as smaller animals such as squirrels and chipmunks. An increasing number of coyotes are feeding off the small game and deer. Ruffed grouse, known in New England as partridges, are plentiful, as are migrating birds such as woodcocks and mourning doves. Wild turkeys, which once thrived in the forests, disappeared in the 1800s. "But they were reintroduced to Rhode Island from Vermont in 1980, and now there are around three thousand birds," says Tefft proudly.

Chipmunks, as well as many other small animals, roam through the state's forests and yards.

Ruffed grouse thrive in Rhode Island.

What makes the abundance of forests so surprising is that, with more than 960 people per square mile, Rhode Island is the second most densely populated state, following only New Jersey. Crowding about a million people into 1,045 square miles of land means that the inhabited portions of the state—the parts not occupied by forests or farmland—have undergone a fundamental change in character. Historian William H. Jordy mourned that change, once saying that modern-day Rhode Island has lost "the sense of individual villages and town centers, as the towns have spread into a continuous suburb."

POWERFUL WATERS

Because of its tiny size, every town and village in Rhode Island lies within twenty-five miles of the sea. "Rhode Island is truly an ocean state," wrote newspaperman Stuart Hale. "No resident is more than thirty minutes away by car from the water's edge." It's not surprising that in addition to a state bird, a state flower, and other official symbols, Rhode Island has a state shellfish—a local breed of clam called a quahog.

Digging for clams is a favorite activity along Rhode Island's beaches.

Rhode Island's stunning shoreline has played a key role in the state's increasing tourist trade.

With four hundred miles of coastline, Rhode Island has every variety of shore landscape, from the high, shifting dunes of Watch Hill and the rocky beaches of Little Compton to the broad, flat shores of Newport and Narragansett, which attract huge crowds in the summer.

Water has been the key to the state's prosperity—the salt water of the Atlantic and Narragansett Bay and the freshwater of the rivers and streams that empty into them. The ocean supported the early Rhode Island industries of fishing, boatbuilding, and international trade. The rivers provided power to run the state's first mills. Rhode Island's rivers were particularly valuable because, as one historian noted, they were "fast-moving, almost never frozen, and never dry," and therefore "perfectly adapted for mill wheels to generate steady and certain sources of power." Today, factories no longer depend on water power; like the ocean and the bay, Rhode Island's rivers are mainly used for recreation.

SAVING THE SALT PONDS

The southern edge of Rhode Island is home to an unusual eco-system: a series of saltwater tidal ponds, which New Englanders call salt ponds. Some of these ponds are connected to the ocean but partially sealed off behind long, narrow sandbars; others are closed to the ocean.

While the ponds cover some 3,700 acres, they are only three to seven feet deep. This shallowness allows sunlight to penetrate all the way to the bottom, promoting the growth of eelgrass and other plants and thus forming the perfect environment for many species of fish and shellfish, such as flounder, quahogs, bay scallops, and oysters. Migratory birds often stop at these ponds for shelter and food.

Today Rhode Island's salt ponds are endangered. An oil spill in 1996 polluted five of the ponds, but pollution from homeowners' septic systems is an even greater threat.

Rhode Island's peaceful salt ponds provide a home for many types of fish and shellfish and are important feeding and nesting sites for birds and mammals.

Because of such dangers, local activist Virginia Lee founded the Rhode Island Salt Pond Watchers, who monitor the ponds' health by taking water samples. "We are the Ocean State," she says, "and environmental quality is a big part of the quality of life for Rhode Islanders."

Thanks to information her group provided on dangerous levels of bacteria in the water, one of the ponds and portions of two others have been closed to clam digging, and new septic regulations have

Monitoring by citizen groups has helped keep the salt ponds healthy.

been enacted. Her efforts have inspired similar groups as far away as Texas. "There are over a thousand programs now around the country," she says, in which ordinary citizens—many of them schoolchildren—watch over the quality of the air and water around them.

A CLIMATE BOTH MILD AND STORMY

Over the years, writers have described Rhode Island's climate as everything from "invigorating and changeable" to "even and excellent throughout the year." In truth, Rhode Island has a wide variety of climates for such a small state. The dry winds of the state's interior create a more severe climate than the gentle sea breezes of the coastal regions. Block Island, for example, enjoys an average annual growing season of 214 days, compared with only 144 days for the landlocked town of Kingston. A blizzard in 1978 left ten inches of snow on Block Island—but fifty-six inches in the northern counties. Generally, however, the state's snowfall is light for New England. Unlike their neighbors, Rhode Islanders have only a 25 percent chance of a white Christmas each year. "For New England," says native Rhode Islander John Hale, now living in Maine, "Rhode Island's about as tropical as you can get."

In the summer, sea breezes keep Rhode Island's coastal areas cooler than farther inland. But even inland, the temperature rises above ninety degrees only about eight days each year.

The coast does suffer from the weather in one respect: since 1635, it has been devastated by two dozen major hurricanes and

Although Rhode Island is not as cold as much of New England, sometimes boats still get trapped in the winter ice.

hundreds of smaller storms called northeasters. A fierce hurricane hit in 1938, causing widespread flooding, forty-foot waves, and winds of 120 miles per hour. It was the worst natural disaster in New England history, leaving more than 600 people dead—317 of them were Rhode Islanders. The state suffered more than $100 million in property damage. In downtown Providence, the waters rose to seven feet above street level. Today three massive forty-foot-wide hurricane gates help protect the city, but a number of buildings throughout the state still bear plaques on their outer walls marking the height of the 1938 flood. "Rhode Islanders are proud of their past," says a European engineer now living in Providence, "even their disasters."

2 A TRADITION OF INDEPENDENCE

Rocky Farm and Cherry Neck, Newport, Rhode Island, *by George Champlin Mason*

Although small, Rhode Island is rich in history. The area it now covers was inhabited for thousands of years before the coming of European settlers. Scientists believe that tribes whose ancestors originated in Asia migrated there more than eight thousand years ago.

INDIAN HERITAGE

By the 1600s, when the settlers arrived, perhaps 30,000 Indians lived there in five main tribes: the Niantics, Nipmucks, Pequots, Wampanoags, and Narragansetts. These last two groups were the largest, and they were frequently at war with each other.

Rhode Island's Indians moved often, setting up villages near the shore in summer, where they planted crops and gathered shellfish, and in the forest in winter, where they carved shells into intricately designed beads called wampum, which they exchanged with neighboring tribes. Their homes, designed to be easily taken down and moved, were built of bark, animal skin, or straw mats over a framework of poles tied together at the top, with a smokehole in the roof. Women had the job of erecting and taking down homes and transporting them when the tribe moved.

Women also did the planting and plowing. Corn was their main

The Narragansetts, Wampanoags, and other Indians in the region were expert canoeists.

crop, along with squash and beans. The only crop men grew was tobacco. Each man carried a bag of it around his neck and smoked it in a pipe. Throughout the year, the men hunted and fished. Game was abundant, as were wild berries and edible roots. The Indians made tools and weapons of chipped stone. They built birchbark canoes and sailed in dugouts—canoes made of hollowed-out logs.

EARLY EXPLORATION

No one can be sure exactly when the first Europeans reached the shores of what is now New England. Possibly Viking seafarers from

Norway explored the region as early as A.D. 1000. But the first European known to have set foot in this land was Giovanni da Verrazano, an Italian sailing for France, who explored Narragansett Bay in 1524 while searching for a way to Asia.

Verrazano may have indirectly given the state its name. He is said to have compared one of the local islands—either Aquidneck or, more likely, Block Island—to the Greek island of Rhodes. Today Aquidneck, like the entire state, is called Rhode Island. Other historians say that the name comes from the Dutch trader Adriaen Block, who sailed the region in 1614 and called one of the islands *roodt eylandt*, or "red island," because of its red clay shores. Whether or not he named Rhode Island, he did give his name to one place he visited: Block Island.

FOUNDING A COLONY

Americans sometimes assume that the early colonists left England in search of religious freedom, but the word "freedom" can be misleading. The groups known as the Pilgrims—who settled in Plymouth, Massachusetts, in 1620—and the Puritans—who settled in the Massachusetts Bay area ten years later—sought religious freedom for themselves, not for others. Convinced that their way of worshiping God was the only right way, they were intolerant of anyone who disagreed.

One idealistic young Puritan minister had different ideas. Roger Williams arrived in Boston from England in 1631 and taught at a church in nearby Salem. Unlike his fellow Puritans, he believed in what is called the separation of church and state. Government, he felt, had no business interfering with religion or enforcing religious laws; that made for bad government and bad religion. He argued that it was wrong for the state to compel people to attend church and to honor the Sabbath. "Forced worship stinks in God's nostrils," he said. Religion was a private matter, for each individual to practice as he or she pleased. Williams's independent views, and the courage with which he expressed them, continually got him into trouble.

So did his attitude toward the Indians. From the start, he befriended them, traded with them, studied their language and their customs, and respected them as human beings. "Nature," he wrote, "knows no difference between European and American [Indian] in blood, birth, bodies, etc." What especially angered the Puritan authorities was Williams's declaration that the colonists had no right to the Indians' land.

A natural peacemaker, he became warm friends with Massasoit, the leader of the Wampanoags, based on the eastern side of Narragansett Bay, and with Canonicus, a leader of the Narragansetts, living on the western side. These men saw Williams almost as a son, even though the two tribes were enemies.

In late 1635, Williams learned that the Massachusetts Bay authorities planned to banish him and ship him back to England. With only his faithful servant, Thomas Angell, as a companion, he set forth into the snowy wilderness to find a new home. After fourteen weeks of wandering, they settled at Massasoit's winter camp in what is now Rehoboth, Massachusetts. In the spring, they were joined by Williams's wife and children and a few followers. Forbidden from settling in the area—it belonged to the Plymouth Colony, which feared offending its Massachusetts Bay neighbors—

Roger Williams respected the Indians who lived along Narragansett Bay. In a poem, he once warned his fellow Englishmen, "Be not proud English of thy birth and blood,/Thy brother Indian is by birth as good."

Williams and his party paddled up the Seekonk River, searching for a place to live. They spied a group of Indians on the western shore, who, tradition has it, hailed Williams with the amiable greeting, "What cheer, Netop?" (What news, friend?) They were Narragansetts, who gladly gave Williams land along the river to found a settlement. In thanks for "God's merciful providence," Williams called the place Providence.

A HAVEN FOR MISFITS

The Providence colony—officially known as Providence Plantations—was meant to be, in Williams's words, "a shelter for persons distressed of conscience," a refuge for those who had been persecuted for their beliefs.

Inspired by Williams, religious misfits began moving into other areas along Narragansett Bay. In 1638, another independent-minded Puritan, Anne Hutchinson—who had been banished by the Massachusetts Bay Colony for preaching fiercely against the established church—settled at Portsmouth, at the north end of Aquidneck Island. A year later, William Coddington broke away from Hutchinson and founded a settlement called Newport at the island's southern tip. Another ardent believer in religious liberty, Samuel Gorton, founded a village called Shawomet south of Providence in 1642. Its name was later changed to Warwick. By this time, these towns were thought of as a single unit, "Rhode Island and Providence Plantations." That remains the state's official name today; the smallest state in the Union has the longest name.

Soon the new colony, with its reputation for religious freedom, was attracting groups such as Quakers and Jews who did not feel welcome in the other colonies. In fact, Rhode Island suffered abuse from its less tolerant neighbors. To one minister, the place was "the receptacle of all sorts of riff-raff people, and is nothing else than the sewer of New England." Called an "asylum to evil-doers," it was nicknamed "Rogues' Island."

WAR WITH THE INDIANS

Roger Williams wanted to be "peaceable" neighbors with the Indians. But other colonists, hungry for land, were neither honorable nor neighborly.

By 1674, Massasoit's son, King Philip, had had enough. A third of New England's Indians had been wiped out by disease since the white man had arrived, and his people, the Wampanoags, had suffered more than most. Now they were being crowded off their land by settlers. "Tract after tract is gone," he said. "But a small part of the dominions of my ancestors remains. I am determined not to live till I have no country."

The Wampanoags began preying on homesteaders, murdering, looting, and burning. In 1675, the Massachusetts and Connecticut colonies declared war. Rhode Islanders and Narragansetts tried to stay out of the conflict, known as King Philip's War, but

King Philip led the Wampanoags in an unsuccessful war to keep control of their land.

they were drawn in when soldiers from the other colonies made a surprise raid on the Narragansetts, who they feared might be harboring Philip. In what was called the Great Swamp Fight, the Massachusetts and Connecticut troops attacked the Narragansetts in the Great Swamp west of Kingston, Rhode Island, in December 1675. The camp was burned, and hundreds of Narragansetts were killed, including women, children, and the elderly. Their leader, Canonchet, escaped.

Joining the Wampanoags, the Narragansetts retaliated by ambushing more than seventy white soldiers and their Indian allies near Central Falls, Rhode Island. They then burned Providence and other towns in the area. Many colonists fled to Aquidneck.

Eventually both Canonchet and Philip were captured and shot. Although there were occasional skirmishes later, the Indians had been conquered.

SLAVERS AND SMUGGLERS

Some Indians were shipped to southern colonies or the West Indies as slaves. Rhode Islanders tended to be less tolerant of slavery in their own colony. In 1652 the towns of Warwick and Providence outlawed any human servitude, whether "blacke mankinde or white," lasting more than ten years. This was America's first anti-slavery law. However, it did not remain in effect for long.

In time Newport and Bristol were among the leading slave-holding cities in New England. Slavery in New England was different from slavery in the South. Households that owned slaves typically had only a few, who performed the same range of tasks as white servants. They did not simply work in the fields, as was often the case on southern plantations. They lived closely with the family and adopted the family's customs. Because Puritans thought it important that everyone understand the Bible, slaves were usually taught to read.

From the start, New Englanders had a guilty conscience about slavery. Moses Brown, whose wealthy family was among Providence's most active slave traders, had a change of heart and freed his slaves in 1773. "I am clearly convinced," he wrote, "that the buying and selling of men . . . is contrary to the Divine mind."

In 1784, Rhode Island passed a "gradual emancipation act": present slaves would remain in bondage, but their children would be free. By 1800, less than 1 percent of Rhode Island's population were slaves, and by 1840 there were only five slaves left in the state.

Until the American Revolution, however, merchants and shipowners in Newport and Providence were heavily involved in the so-called triangle trade: rum from the colonies was traded in Africa for slaves, the slaves were traded in the West Indies for molasses; and the molasses was shipped to Rhode Island to be made into rum. By 1750, rum was the colony's major manufactured item. Fishing, especially whaling, was its other important industry.

In the 1760s, England passed a series of taxes that restricted trade between the colonies and non-British islands in the West Indies. Deprived of molasses from islands owned by France, Spain, and Holland, Rhode Islanders took to smuggling. In 1764, Rhode Island troops fired on a British ship hunting for smugglers as it attempted to leave Newport harbor. Some believe these were the first shots of the Revolution.

Moses Brown, one of Providence's leading citizens, was once a slave trader.

Slave auctions were once common in Newport, a center of the slave trade in the eighteenth century.

Newport, July 6, 1764.

Juſt imported in the Sloop *Elizabeth,* from *Africa,* and to be ſold, by

John Miller,

At his Houſe, or Store ;

A Number of healthy

Negro Boys and Girls.

Likewiſe to be ſold,——*Tillock's* and *Kip-pen's* Snuff, by the Caſk or Dozen.

A more famous incident eight years later has also been called the first act of the Revolution. On June 9, 1772, a British ship, the *Gaspee*, ran aground in Narragansett Bay while pursuing a Rhode Island boat suspected of smuggling. Late that night, eight boats manned by citizens of Providence attacked the ship. After shooting the *Gaspee*'s captain, the men boarded the ship, forced the crew into boats, and set the ship ablaze. The wounded captain was rowed to a house onshore. "Bloodstains on the floor," wrote historian William G. McLoughlin, "were pointed out for a century thereafter as 'the first blood of the Revolution.'"

The destruction of the British ship the Gaspee *in 1772 was one of the first acts of rebellion by American colonists.*

FIRST TO REBEL

Because Rhode Islanders were so heavily involved in trade, British trade restrictions and taxes affected them severely. This made them eager to be free of Great Britain's rule—so eager, in fact, that the colony's general assembly voted to end its allegiance to England on May 4, 1776, two full months before the other twelve colonies declared their independence. (May 4 is now celebrated as Rhode Island Independence Day.)

For all its eagerness to fight, the colony saw only one major battle during the Revolution, the Battle of Rhode Island. In August 1778, American troops under General John Sullivan attacked the British forces occupying Newport. They fought the British back to the final defenses around Newport, but they were not able to capture the city. The Americans withdrew, pursued by the British. At Portsmouth they successfully fended off a British attack and were able to retreat to safety. A battalion of freed slaves, the Black Regiment, fought courageously for the colonists and helped keep the British at bay. It was the first such regiment to see combat in America.

THE INDUSTRIAL REVOLUTION

After the war, Rhode Island maintained its independent spirit. It refused to ratify the United States Constitution until ten amendments—the Bill of Rights—were added. At a special convention in May 1790, it finally voted to join the Union, the last of the original thirteen colonies to do so. The motion passed by only two votes.

THE BOMBARDMENT OF BRISTOL

On October 7, 1775, a small British fleet commanded by Captain James Wallace approached Bristol in search of supplies for the main fleet anchored in Newport harbor. After a bombardment lasting an hour and a half, Captain Wallace presented his demands: two hundred sheep and thirty cattle. After some negotiation, the matter was settled with the delivery of only forty sheep.

In sev-en-teen hun-dred sev-en-ty five, Our Bris-tol town was much sur-prised, By a thiev-ing

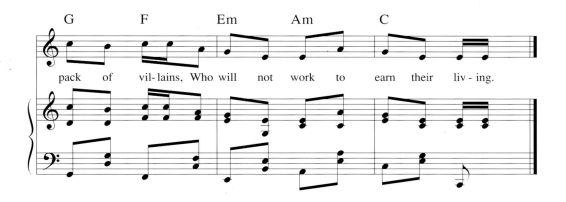

pack of vil-lains, Who will not work to earn their liv - ing.

October, 'twas the seventh day,
As I have heard the people say,
Wallace—his name be ever cursed,
Come on our harbor just at dusk.

And there his ship did safely moor,
And quickly sent his barge ashore,
With orders that should not be broke,
Or that we might expect a smoke.

Demanding that our magistrates
Should quickly come on board his ship,
And let him have some sheep and cattle,
Or that they might expect a battle.

At eight o'clock by signal given,
Our peaceful atmosphere was riven;
Women with children in their arms,
With doleful cries ran to the farms.

With all their firing and their skill,
They did not any person kill,
Neither was any person hurt,
Except the Reverend Parson Burt.

And he was not killed by a ball,
As judged by jurors one and all,
But being in a sickly state,
He frightened fell, which proved his fate.

Another truth to you I'll tell,
That you may see they leveled well,
For aiming for to kill the people,
They fired their first shot into a steeple.

They fired low, they fired high,
The women scream, the children cry,
And all their firing and their racket
Shot off the topmast of a packet!

That same year, 1790, marked the birth of America's industrial revolution. The birthplace was Pawtucket, Rhode Island, where an English immigrant named Samuel Slater set up America's first successful water-powered cotton mill.

Slater, though a clever man, had not invented this process. That honor went to another Englishman, Sir Richard Arkwright, who had built a machine for spinning cotton into yarn. The English were so determined to keep the design to themselves that they passed laws preventing any craftspeople with knowledge of the machinery from leaving the country. Of course, it is practically

The American industrial revolution began in Pawtucket, Rhode Island, when Samuel Slater built a cotton mill that took advantage of the raging torrent of the Blackstone River.

DORR'S REBELLION—A SECOND AMERICAN REVOLUTION

Although Roger Williams was a staunch believer in democracy, Rhode Island lagged behind the other colonies in granting citizens the right to vote. For much of its history, only adult white male property owners and their eldest sons could vote—which left out more than half the adult white males, to say nothing of nonwhites and women.

Thomas Wilson Dorr, a wealthy lawyer, considered this a great injustice to working people. In 1841, he formed a political party, the People's Party, dedicated to winning the vote for all men. The party held its own election, allowing all white males to vote. (Dorr wanted blacks to be included, but was overruled.) The party adopted a new state constitution and elected Dorr governor of Rhode Island. He was inaugurated in May 1842 in Providence—one day before the legal governor, Samuel Ward King, was inaugurated in Newport. Tiny Rhode Island now had two governors!

The official government refused to recognize this upstart. The People's Party tried to seize the Providence arsenal, where weapons were stored, but troops chased them away. Dorr then attempted to raise a revolutionary army. When he failed to attract enough support, he gave himself up and eventually spent a year in jail.

But his message had been heard. Thanks to Dorr's Rebellion, Rhode Island granted the vote to all adult males, black and white, making it the only state before the Civil War where blacks and whites could vote as equals. Women, though, would have to wait another eighty years.

impossible to keep an idea from getting out. Slater had worked in one of Arkwright's mills for seven years and had carefully memorized the design. Dressed as a farmer, he had slipped out of the country illegally, knowing he could make his fortune.

By 1815, Rhode Island had a hundred cotton mills, and two-thirds of the state's villages had mills on their rivers. "The nation's Industrial Revolution was powered by *our* rivers," boasts journalist David Brussat. Rivers were dammed and reservoirs constructed to maintain a constant supply of water.

In Providence in 1827, Slater established the first steam-driven cotton mill. Soon steam power had replaced water power; factories could now be set up anywhere, not just on rivers, and could operate year-round. By 1860, half the state's workers were employed in manufacturing, while only 10 percent worked on farms and 3 percent in fishing. Rhode Island had become the most industrialized state in the nation.

This was long before the era of child labor laws, and the majority of the mill workers were children as young as eight years old. For them, schooling became a remote possibility once they joined the workforce. Most of the adult workers were women. Both women and children worked for lower wages than men.

The first half of the nineteenth century saw a growing division in America between the industrialized Northern states—which one by one outlawed slavery—and the Southern states, where wealthy landowners depended on slaves to work their fields. In 1861, the dispute over slavery led the Southern states to withdraw from the Union, and the Civil War began.

As a center of industry, Rhode Island profited greatly from this war. Its factories worked overtime turning out cannons, rifles, and other weapons; its mills produced textiles for military uniforms, blankets, and tents. Patriotic feelings were strong—the state contributed 24,000 men to the Union cause, 5,000 more than the government had requested.

After the war, another type of manufacturing gained importance in Providence: the metals industry. By 1900, the city was trumpeting its Five Industrial Wonders of the World, for within its borders stood the world's largest tool factory, file factory, steam engine factory, screw factory, and silverware factory. The city also became famous for its jewelry.

MODERN TIMES

By the early 1900s, Rhode Island's cotton mills were beginning to close, as businesses relocated to the South, where taxes were lower and labor cheaper. Textiles remained the state's principal industry, but the boom years were over.

When the stock market crashed in 1929, millions of Americans were thrown out of work in the resulting Great Depression. But hard times had hit Rhode Island years earlier. Throughout the 1930s, mills continued to close. By 1937, nearly 80 percent of the cotton mills that had been operating in 1923 were gone.

With jobs scarce, people had to make do with less. Some found work at lower wages; some struggled to survive on part-time work. Many hungry Rhode Islanders depended on charities. Seafood—relatively cheap and plentiful in the Ocean State—became the staple diet for many Rhode Islanders. One woman recalls eating

Many women worked in Rhode Island's thriving textile factories. Here they are preparing cotton thread.

so many lobsters during these years that she would never touch another one.

What pulled Rhode Island—and the rest of America—out of the depression was World War II. As they had in the Civil War, Rhode Island's industries turned out goods needed for the war effort. But when the war ended in 1945, factories closed. More mills moved south.

Yet today, Rhode Island is prospering again. One reason is that its economy has diversified. Although manufacturing is still important, service industries, such as banking, insurance, and health care, have grown. Another reason is the state's quality of life. As one historian wrote, "Life in Rhode Island is less hectic and more pleasant than in Boston or New York; and one is only minutes away from ocean beaches and forests." Rhode Island, which lost population in the 1970s, is once again a place where people want to live.

It's also a place that people want to visit. Though always a vacation spot because of its beaches, it has learned in recent decades to honor and preserve its past. Samuel Slater's cotton mill in Pawtucket is now a museum, and Providence has turned itself into a kind of living museum, with entire neighborhoods reflecting its colonial heritage. Throughout the state, there's a new understanding that one of Rhode Island's most valuable assets— the secret of its appeal and the source of its charm—is its history.

3 POWER AND MONEY

The capitol in Providence

The center of Rhode Island's government is the beautiful white marble capitol in Providence. At the top of its dome stands a twelve-foot bronze statue known as the Independent Man, a symbol of the Rhode Island spirit. (Originally the statue was to be of Roger Williams, but no pictures exist to show what he looked like.)

Providence was not always Rhode Island's only seat of government. Until 1854, Providence, Newport, East Greenwich, Bristol, and South Kingstown all served as capitals, and legislators traveled from one to the other so that no single region would be favored. No other state has ever had five capitals! In 1854, the number was reduced to two—Providence and Newport—and in 1900 Providence became the sole capital.

INSIDE GOVERNMENT

Rhode Island's government is modeled on the nation's, with three main divisions, each with its own power and responsibilities, each serving to balance the others.

Executive. The head of the executive branch is the governor, who is elected to a four-year term. The governor prepares the state budget and accepts or rejects bills passed by the legislature. If the governor signs a bill, it becomes law. If he or she vetoes, or rejects, the bill, it does not.

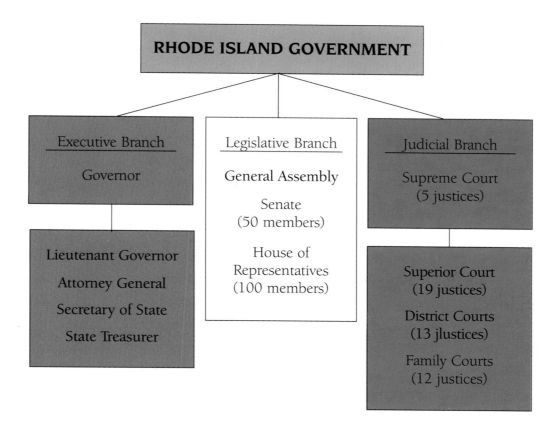

RHODE ISLAND GOVERNMENT

Executive Branch

Governor

Lieutenant Governor

Attorney General

Secretary of State

State Treasurer

Legislative Branch

General Assembly

Senate
(50 members)

House of
Representatives
(100 members)

Judicial Branch

Supreme Court
(5 justices)

Superior Court
(19 justices)

District Courts
(13 jlustices)

Family Courts
(12 justices)

Other important executive branch officials are the lieutenant governor, the secretary of state, the attorney general, and the general treasurer. These officials are elected independently, so it is possible for the governor and lieutenant governor to come from different political parties.

Legislative. Like the U.S. Congress, Rhode Island's legislature—known as the general assembly—is made up of a senate and a house of representatives. The fifty senators and one hundred representatives are all elected for two-year terms.

In the general assembly, bills are introduced and voted on. If a bill passes, it goes to the governor for approval. If the governor vetoes it, a three-fifths majority in both houses can override the decision and turn it into law. The general assembly also votes on whether to approve the budget that the governor proposes each year.

Judicial. The judicial branch rules on legal matters and decides whether the other two branches have acted according to the law. Rhode Island's highest court, the supreme court, has five justices who are appointed for life. Until 1994, these judges were chosen by the general assembly—a system that invited corruption, since the assembly usually gave the jobs to fellow legislators. As a result, the judicial branch of government was not really independent of the legislative branch. Today, supreme court justices are appointed by the governor, who selects from a small group of candidates rated "highly qualified" by an independent commission. The choices must be approved by both chambers of the assembly.

The governor also appoints judges to five lower courts: the superior court and, below that, district court, family court, traffic court, and workers' compensation court. These appointments must be approved by the senate.

SHIFTING POWER

The twentieth century saw a great change in Rhode Island: a shift in political power from Republicans to Democrats, from old-line Yankee Protestants to newly arrived Catholic immigrants.

What is a Yankee? To someone from another country, a Yankee is anyone from the United States. To someone from a southern state, a Yankee is a northerner. But in the North itself, "Yankee" means a traditional New Englander whose ancestors came from England or Scotland.

Until the turn of the century, Rhode Island was controlled by the descendants of its early English settlers—by Yankees. They ran the businesses and newspapers, they had the most money, and they held most political offices. Most were staunch Republicans. But eventually immigrants from countries such as Ireland, Italy, Portugal, and France began to outnumber this older segment of the population. By the mid-1930s, these more recent arrivals and their descendants, who generally voted Democratic, were able to get elected to positions of power. Even though some Republicans have been elected governor, since 1935 Democrats have dominated Rhode Island politics and have never lost control of the general assembly. Some people estimate that 85 percent of the votes in the assembly are nearly unanimous.

POWER CORRUPTS

When one party so thoroughly dominates, the result is often corruption. When the Republicans controlled Rhode Island, they had been accused of vote-buying and other shady practices designed to enrich themselves and maintain their political power. The Democrats, when they took over, were accused of the same.

Until recently, Rhode Island was sometimes called the most corrupt state in the Union, and there was some truth to the charge. Bribery, misuse of funds, and the use of political office for personal gain were common. If you wanted to obtain a favor from a state senator, or do business with a city, or influence the outcome of a trial, you paid a bribe. Since 1986, two chief justices of the Rhode Island Supreme Court have resigned in disgrace; a

EARNING A LIVING

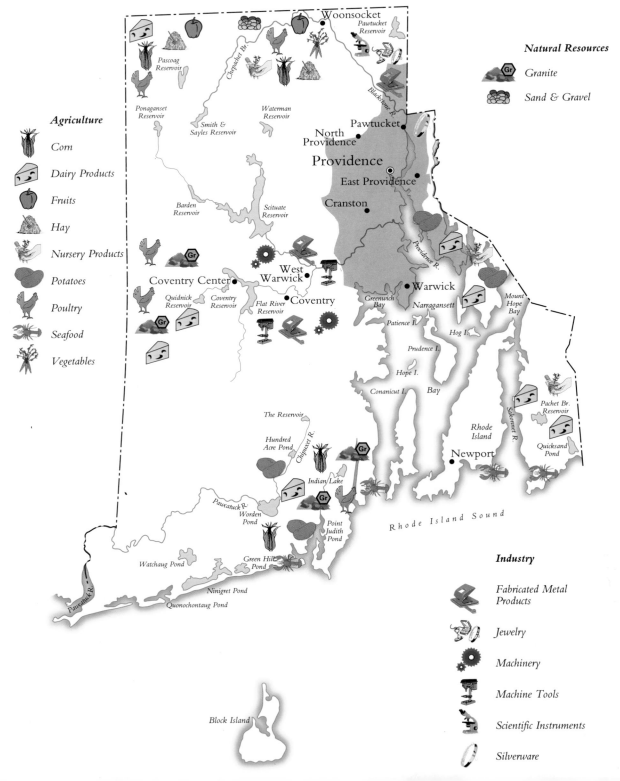

Natural Resources

Granite

Sand & Gravel

Agriculture

Corn

Dairy Products

Fruits

Hay

Nursery Products

Potatoes

Poultry

Seafood

Vegetables

Industry

Fabricated Metal Products

Jewelry

Machinery

Machine Tools

Scientific Instruments

Silverware

superior court judge was arrested for taking a bribe; and two mayors were convicted of corrupt activities. The worst scandal broke in 1990, when a prominent banker fled with $13 million from a bank that insured the funds in other banks. As a result, forty-five banks and credit unions had to close temporarily, keeping more than 200,000 depositors from their accounts.

What caused this corruption? Some point to the dominance of one party, which has allowed legislators to ignore the law without fear of being voted out of office. Another factor has been the presence of organized crime. Until recently, the state was widely regarded as the New England headquarters of the Mafia. The state's small size has also contributed to the problem, by making it easier for friends to help one another evade the law.

H. Philip West, executive director of Common Cause of Rhode Island, an organization dedicated to honesty in government, says that thanks to "massive public indignation" over recent scandals, the state has seen "profound changes that have been enacted with vast public support." In 1994, for example, 70 percent of voters approved the selection of all state judges based on merit. Today, says West, Rhode Island benefits from "radical new ethics laws and the strongest ethics commission in the United States. It has been a dramatic change, and it is working—not perfectly, but it is working."

WEALTH FROM THE EARTH AND SEA

Rhode Island is not especially rich in mineral resources. Although the state has some coal, its main minerals are limestone, granite, sand, and gravel, all of which are used in construction.

Although few farms remain in Rhode Island, some fine old barns are still standing.

More important to the state is its fertile soil. Although housing has overtaken most of Rhode Island's farmland, potatoes, corn, and apples are still grown in the Narragansett Bay area. Fewer than forty dairy farms remain in the state, although there are now some llama farms.

The state bird, the hardy Rhode Island Red chicken, was developed in the 1850s near Adamsville. Today, the town has a granite marker proclaiming this fact—America's only monument to a chicken. No longer raised as widely as it once was, the bird is still popular among Rhode Islanders: "Loud, inbred, and confined to a small place, he is the perfect representative for our people," jokes local writer Ted Widmer.

Rhode Islanders have long looked to the sea for prosperity from trade and fishing. The state continues to serve as a center for imports and exports, and much of New England's oil passes through the port of Providence. But less than a thousand Rhode

Rhode Island Red chickens were developed in the state that gave them their name.

Islanders remain fishermen, with 1,500 more employed in other aspects of the fishing industry. The most common catches are lobster, cod, scrod, flounder, hake, scup, whiting, mackerel, and herring.

MANUFACTURING FOR THE NATION

Today, Rhode Island's economy relies on manufacturing. But while it is the state's largest source of jobs, it employs only around a quarter of all Rhode Island workers, whereas fifty years ago it employed half.

Rhode Island factories produce electrical goods, precision tools, pens, luggage, furniture, glass, and various paper, chemical, plastic, leather, and rubber products. But the state's leading manufacturing industry is jewelry and silverware production. Rhode Island factories specialize in costume jewelry—earrings, pins, watch-bands, necklaces, and rings, mass-produced and relatively low-priced. It's been estimated that 85 percent of such jewelry manufactured in the United States is made in the Providence area.

That sounds impressive, but in truth the industry has been hurt in recent years. Increasingly, costume jewelry is being imported from China and other Asian nations, where it can be manufactured at a fraction of the cost. And some Chinese factories are counter-feiting Rhode Island–made jewelry, including the brand names, flooding the United States market with cheap imitations that

Fishing is an important industry in the Ocean State. Inset: Lobster is one of the many types of shellfish that can be caught off of Rhode Island's shores.

Providence has been a center of silverware production for more than a century.

people mistake for the genuine product. As a result, some Rhode Island jewelry factories have closed, and others are struggling to survive. "Several years ago a major American company offered to buy 100,000 corporate medallions from me if I could match, or even come close to, the unit prices they cost in Taiwan: twelve to fourteen cents each," says a retired Rhode Island jewelry executive. "I contacted nearly a dozen firms in Providence, and the cheapest price they could quote me was twenty-eight cents." That inability to compete, he says, is Rhode Island's jewelry industry's largest problem.

One of Rhode Island's great success stories has been the Hasbro toy company, the second-largest toymaker in the world, which has its headquarters in Pawtucket. Hasbro is short for the *Has*senfeld *bro*thers, Henry and Halel, immigrants from Eastern Europe who, in 1924, opened a shop in Providence selling textile remnants—leftover pieces of cloth. They began turning some of their remnants into cloth-covered pencil boxes. Later, the company manufactured play doctor's and nurse's kits. Hasbro hit the big time in 1952 with Mr. Potato Head, the first toy ever advertised on television, and now makes many of America's favorite playthings, including Raggedy Ann, Spirograph, Tinkertoys, Tonka Trucks, G.I. Joe, Lincoln Logs, Play-Doh, Nerf, games such as Scrabble, Monopoly, and Clue, and an ever-growing number of Star Wars toys. Still

GROSS STATE PRODUCT: $37.1 BILLION

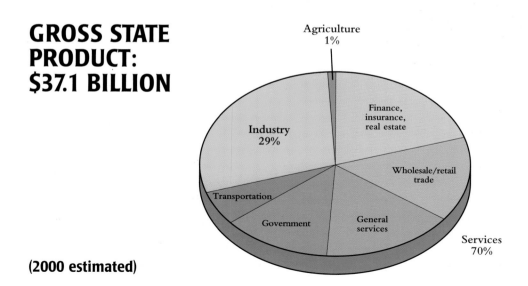

Agriculture 1%

Finance, insurance, real estate

Industry 29%

Wholesale/retail trade

Transportation

Government

General services

Services 70%

(2000 estimated)

a family-run business with $3 billion in sales, Hasbro employs ten thousand people around the world.

THE SERVICE ECONOMY

Over the past half century, the service industry has become increasingly important to Rhode Island's economy. After jewelry manufacturing, in fact, the most common jobs in Rhode Island are in two service industries, tourism and health care. Today, tourism

Newport bustles with tourists who come to enjoy its historic buildings and quaint shops.

NIGHT OWLS

Anyone who's ever eaten in an all-night diner owes thanks to Walter Scott, who invented this most American of restaurants in Providence in 1872. Aware that most restaurants closed at eight, Scott loaded a horse-drawn wagon with pies, sandwiches, and coffee to sell to hungry workers on the night shift. The idea caught on all over New England, and wagons like Scott's, known as "night owls," were soon serving other sorts of food as well, including hot dogs, beans, and cold cuts. By 1880, there were thirty in Providence alone, and by 1917 there were fifty.

With the twentieth century, night owls became motorized, and later, instead of traveling to their customers, they became stationary, like other restaurants. They began to resemble streamlined railroad cars, like the beautiful Modern Diner in Pawtucket, Rhode Island, the first diner ever listed in the National Register of Historic Places. But in Providence, the diner's birthplace—where a diner museum is in the works—a beloved night owl called Haven Brothers still motors through downtown every afternoon at 4:30 P.M. and parks near city hall, serving franks and beans to hungry Rhode Islanders, before disappearing at dawn.

brings more than $1.6 billion yearly to Rhode Island and supports over 25,000 jobs. "If it weren't for tourists, I wouldn't survive," says a Providence bookseller.

Companies in service industries such as banking and insurance have relocated to Rhode Island because the cost of doing business is lower there—as is the cost of living for employees. Providence, in particular, is viewed as a good place to locate a business. "It's between New York and Boston," explains one executive, "so we are near the international financial centers, but we are not burdened by the choking influence of a large city."

GRADING EDUCATION

One key to competing economically with other states—and to attracting both businesses and individuals—is the quality of public education. Rhode Island's record in this area shows some problems.

Education is a top concern for many Rhode Islanders.

Although in 1997, Rhode Island students scored near the national averages in both math and verbal skills, many parents are worried about misbehavior in the classroom. They want schools to get tough with troublemakers who disrupt the class. And they are very keen— more so than most Americans—on community service as a part of education. "It gets the kids involved in the community, it gives them something to do, and it gives them something to be proud of," says a mother with a son and daughter in school. "For some kids, it might be the only thing they can do that they feel good about, confident about. I feel strongly about community service."

But some Rhode Islanders—including Gary Sasse, a prominent businessman and advisor to the governor—worry about whether Rhode Island students will be strong enough to compete in the world economy. "Average won't be good enough in the next century," he says.

4 A MILLION RHODE ISLANDERS

had an almost foreign flavor. As late as the 1960s, "you needed a passport to come to Fox Point," jokes Harry Adler, who runs a hardware store there. "People talked about 'crossing the border' into the neighborhood."

Today, many young people of Portuguese descent have left the neighborhood. The old houses have become more expensive, and many are rented out to students from nearby Brown University. But a Portuguese influence is still visible in annual events such as the church-sponsored Holy Ghost Parade each spring, where parish-

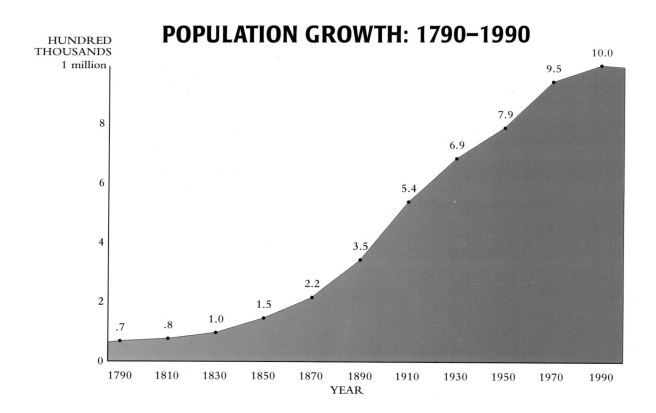

POPULATION GROWTH: 1790–1990

MURDER IN THE TAVERN: A FOLKTALE

Sometimes called "Rogues' Island" by its neighbors, Rhode Island has long had a reputation as a place that harbored misfits and criminals. One such man, Jim Andrews, ran a tavern in the early 1800s, where, so the tale goes, he made lots of money—literally. He was a counterfeiter who employed peddlers traveling throughout the state to pass his phony bills.

One night one of his men burst into the tavern. "The law's after me!" he said. Fearing the man would reveal their scam to the authorities, Andrews poured him drink after drink until the man dropped off to sleep. Andrews then silenced him forever by hammering a huge spike through his neck. He buried the body in a nearby swamp. Later, when two boys almost stumbled over the grave, he dug up the body and reburied it behind the tavern.

It's said that afterward, on dark nights, people passing the tavern would be stopped by a ghostly stranger who would beg them to help pull the spike from his neck.

Years later, after the tavern was long gone, a boy and his mother were passing the same spot on a moonlit winter's night when newly fallen snow covered the ground. Suddenly they made out a shadowy figure walking ahead of them, tugging at something in his neck. They lost sight of the figure, and when they looked down to see where he'd been walking, they could find no footprints in the snow.

ioners bearing flowers and dressed in white, as if for a wedding, march proudly down Wickenden Street, and the Cape Verdean Independence Day Festival each July, when India Point Park is filled with music and food from Cape Verde. Delicious Portuguese bread,

Many Portuguese immigrants have settled in Providence's Fox Point neighborhood.

as sweet as coffee cake, is popular throughout the state. Portuguese is still spoken in many homes in Rhode Island.

New immigrant groups continue to add to the variety that is Rhode Island. In recent years, Vietnamese, Cambodians, and people from the Dominican Republic and various African nations have settled in the state, seeking a better life. "You cannot tell Rhode Islanders that the American Dream doesn't work," the historian William McLoughlin once said. "They have seen it work—not for all, but for enough; not always to the top, but a long way up, compared to life in the Old Country."

Because of the many immigrants from Ireland, Italy, French Canada, and Portugal, as well as Poles who settled in the Central Falls area, by 1910 the majority of Rhode Islanders were Roman Catholics. Since the 1950s a growing Hispanic population has added to the Catholic majority. Today, between 65 and 70 percent of Rhode Islanders are Catholic, making it the most Catholic state in the country. Some Rhode Islanders tend to think in terms of parishes, the area of their local church, rather than counties, towns, or neighborhoods. According to one Rhode Islander, during her childhood, "'Out of parish' was as foreign as 'outtastate.'"

ETHNIC RHODE ISLAND

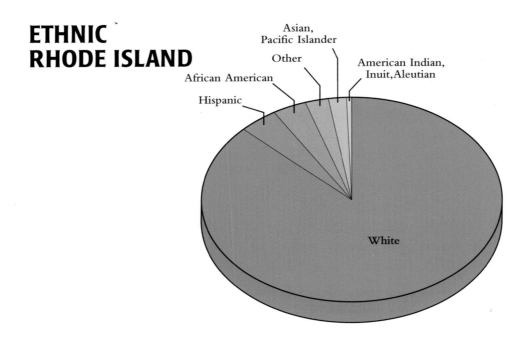

Asian, Pacific Islander
Other
African American
Hispanic
American Indian, Inuit, Aleutian
White

THE TALK OF RHODE ISLAND

"One of the wonders of our state," a Rhode Island magazine once bragged, "is how a place so tiny can hold so many different accents." But while a native Rhode Islander may be able to pick out these regional differences, most outsiders hear a single, very distinctive way of speaking throughout the state.

All over the East Coast, many people drop the *r* in words, pronouncing it more like "ah." But in Rhode Island this tendency is often more extreme; sometimes *r* sounds like a cross between *w* and *v*. In a light-hearted study of Rhode Island speech, language expert Elaine Chaika offered these pronunciations:

area = *eahvia*
bottle = *bah'il*
farmer = *fahma*
four = *faw*
here = *heah*
market = *mocket*
never = *neva*
park = *pahk* or *pock*
parlor = *pala*
partner = *potna*
pure = *pyaw*
short = *shawt*

In his humorous *Rhode Island Dictionary*, Mark Patinkin adds that a Rhode Island auto mechanic may charge you for "pots and layba" (parts and labor), a Rhode Island lifeguard may warn you to be careful of the "shock" (shark), and a Rhode Island house may have a "coppit" (carpet) on the floor.

A growing number of nonwhites adds to the mix that is Rhode Island.

THE JEWISH MIGRATIONS

Jews have lived in Rhode Island since colonial days. Like many other groups, they were attracted by the colony's religious tolerance. The first Jews in Rhode Island arrived in the 1650s. Settling mainly in Newport, they became tailors, merchants, candle makers, soap makers, and traders. There, in 1759, they began building Touro Synagogue, the first synagogue in the colony. Still in use today, it is the oldest surviving Jewish house of worship in North America. Many more Jews arrived in Rhode Island in the 1880s and 1890s. They settled mainly in Providence, where they became shopkeepers or

Touro Synagogue, completed in 1763, is the oldest Jewish house of worship in North America.

garment workers. Though Jews are a small segment of Rhode Island's population today, they are active in the arts, education, business, and politics.

AFRICAN AMERICANS

Blacks, too, make up a relatively small part of the population—less than 4 percent—and they, too, have been present in Rhode

JONNYCAKES

The pancakes known as "jonnycakes"—or, as they were called in colonial days, "journey cakes" (because they were made to take on journeys)—can be made from various kinds of cornmeal, but ideally you should use a rare type of stone-ground cornmeal called Rhode Island Whitecap Flint Corn, which is grown only in the southern part of the state. Have an adult help you with this recipe:

7 tablespoons of cornmeal
1 level tablespoon of sugar
½ teaspoon of salt
½ cup of milk

Place the cornmeal, sugar, and salt in a bowl and pour boiling water over them to scald the meal. Beat the mixture to a smooth consistency, then beat in the milk.

Grease a heated griddle well, drop the batter by spoonfuls on the griddle, and fry until golden brown on each side.

If you like your pancakes thin, press each cake down firmly with a spatula. If you like them thick, do not press them at all.

Island since colonial times. Before the Revolution, most were slaves, but a few were free.

Slavery was dying out in Rhode Island by 1800, but freed blacks were still treated as social outcasts. They were forced into separate schools and churches, and banned from theaters, stagecoaches, and railroad cars. Many were harassed by rowdy whites. "If you were well dressed they would insult you for that, and if you were ragged you would surely be insulted for being so; be as peaceable as you could be, there was no shield for you," recalled William J. Brown, the descendant of slaves owned by Moses Brown, a leading Providence citizen.

The state's African-American population rose after the Civil War when blacks migrated to New England from the South. By the 1900s, most blacks in Rhode Island were transplanted southerners, not the descendants of New England blacks.

INDIANS TODAY

Most Rhode Islanders who describe themselves as Narragansetts are probably also part black, for during the nineteenth century, many members of the two groups intermarried. As early as 1833, few pure-blooded Narragansetts remained. Most of them lived on a nine-square-mile reservation in Charlestown, along Rhode Island's southern coast, until 1880, when they sold the land to the state and the tribe was declared legally "extinct." In 1934, the Narragansetts redeclared their tribal identity, and in 1978 some of their land was returned to them. Today, Indians make up less than one-half of one percent of the state's population.

The Narragansetts celebrate their heritage at powwows and other festivals.

Many of them gather each August on the grounds of Charlestown's Old Indian Church for a two-day tribal meeting and powwow, with outdoor feasting, displays of Indian crafts, and dancing in traditional dress. The festival's sponsors claim it is America's oldest annual event, dating back more than three hundred years.

Something else survives as well: dozens of Rhode Island towns and villages have Indian names, and so do some of the state's major rivers, such as the Pawtuxet, Sakonnet, Seekonk, Woonasquatucket, Moshassuck, and Pawcatuck.

5 SUCCESS STORIES

In centuries past, Rhode Islanders have appeared to the world as farmers, fishermen, resourceful seagoing traders, and shrewd businessmen. But the people of this state have made their marks in other fields as well. Here are a few notable successes.

FANTASTIC IMAGINATIONS

There's something about living in the smallest state that seems to stretch a writer's imagination—as if the state's narrow boundaries force creative people to search for space inside their own heads.

"Rhode Island is the nation's best-kept secret," says Providence resident Paul Di Filippo, whose cutting-edge science fiction has earned him a cult following. "It's an excellent place for a writer like me. There just seems to be something in the air. After all, Pawtucket, a few miles up the river, is the birthplace of our industrial revolution. Maybe that's why the state seems so hospitable to fiction about the effects of technology."

Fantasy fiction has deep roots in Rhode Island. Edgar Allan Poe, America's first great writer of fantastic tales of mystery and terror, came to Providence in 1848 to court the wealthy widow Sarah Helen Whitman, a well-regarded poet who was a fan of Poe's. Reading his famous poem "The Raven" and frightening stories such as "The Masque of the Red Death" and "The Pit and the

Sarah Helen Whitman was fascinated by the macabre tales of Edgar Allan Poe.

Edgar Allan Poe moved to Providence to court Sarah Helen Whitman. In his poem "To Helen," he praised "the poetry of thy presence."

Pendulum," she confessed to a friend, at first gave her "a sensation of such intense horror that I dared neither look at anything he had written nor even utter his name." Soon, however, she found herself excitedly reading "every line that fell from his pen." In Providence, Poe and Whitman talked of love and literature and strolled among the graves at Swan Point Cemetery. But their romance was doomed. Sarah had heard too many rumors about Poe's drinking, and she suspected (correctly) that he was partly attracted to her money. Poe left Providence early in 1849 and by that fall was dead.

Poe's most important successor—and one of America's greatest horror writers—was a lifelong resident of Providence born in 1890 named Howard Phillips Lovecraft. Like Poe, he wrote fantasy and science fiction, as well as poetry.

H. P. Lovecraft was a true Rhode Island eccentric. He lived a fairly solitary life in Providence. He often stayed up all night writing stories, though most of his working hours were spent writing letters to friends. It is estimated that he wrote more than 100,000 letters, some as long as fifty pages. He traveled as far as Louisiana and Quebec, visiting fellow writers and studying architecture, but his most memorable traveling was done in his dreams, which were often sources for his horror stories. He specialized in a new and original kind of horror in which recognizable New England villages are menaced by monstrous alien creatures from other dimensions. "When Lovecraft was on the money—as in 'The Dunwich Horror,' 'The Rats in the Walls,' and best of all, 'The Colour Out of Space'— his stories packed an incredible wallop," says modern horror master Stephen King. "The best of them make us feel the size of the

I AM PROVIDENCE

"I am Providence," H. P. Lovecraft once wrote a friend, "and Providence is myself." Lovecraft set many of his stories in the streets and houses of his beloved Providence. In *The Case of Charles Dexter Ward*, he describes the hero's return to the city in 1926:

The entry to Providence along Reservoir and Elmwood avenues was a breathless and wonderful thing. . . . At the high square where Broad, Weybosset, and Empire Streets join, he saw before and below him in the fire of sunset the pleasant, remembered houses and domes and steeples of the old town; and his head swam curiously as the vehicle rolled down to the terminal behind the Biltmore [Hotel], bringing into view the great dome and soft, roof-pierced greenery of the ancient hill across the river, and the tall colonial spire of the First Baptist Church . . . pink in the magic evening light. . . .

Old Providence! It was this place and the mysterious forces of its long, continuous history which had brought him into being.

universe we hang suspended in, and suggest shadowy forces that could destroy us all."

MEMORABLE VISIONS

When Americans think of George Washington, they usually think of the portrait of him by Rhode Island artist Gilbert Stuart. Painted in 1796, it is, according to historian Thomas Craven, "the most famous picture in American art." Stuart himself wrote: "It was whispered about that I fixed on Washington because I needed the money. How true! I was as broke as last year's bird's nest, but that

Notoriously slow at painting, Gilbert Stuart took eighteen years to complete his portrait of former first lady Abigail Adams. "There is no knowing how to take hold of this man, nor by what means to prevail upon him to fulfill his engagements," she wrote.

isn't all. I believed that Washington was the greatest man in history, and I'm not too modest to say that I was the only artist capable of doing him justice." The portrait proved so popular that Stuart painted 130 more just like it. He also painted portraits of presidents John Adams, Thomas Jefferson, James Madison, and James Monroe, making himself eighteenth-century America's most celebrated painter. His birthplace is now a museum.

Today Rhode Island is home to two of the country's most popular artists for young people, Chris Van Allsburg and David Macaulay. Though each has his own special style and vision of the world, they have a few things in common. Both have taught at Providence's Rhode Island School of Design, both have written and illustrated books that won the Caldecott Medal for the best children's picture book of the year, both have produced strings of best-sellers—and through it all, they've remained friends.

Chris Van Allsburg is among America's most celebrated children's authors and illustrators. *The Polar Express*, in which a small boy takes a magical nighttime train journey to Santa's city at the North Pole, is a Christmas classic. His equally magical *Jumanji* was made into a hit movie filled with hilarious and hair-raising special effects. A lesser-known book, but perhaps even more wonderful, is *The Mysteries of Harris Burdick.*

Journeys to the North Pole are not for Van Allsburg, who lives in Providence. "I don't like to travel," he says. But it's clear that like Lovecraft, Van Allsburg travels widely in his head. "Some people have a more active imagination than others," he says, "and when you have an *over*active imagination, you either succeed as an artist . . . or they send you away!"

"The idea of the extra-ordinary happening in the context of the ordinary is what's kind of fascinating to me," Chris Van Allsburg once said.

"I am someone who in his work has always tried to walk the line between entertaining and informing," says artist, writer, and architect David Macaulay.

If Van Allsburg is known for his flights of fancy, the books by his friend David Macaulay are more down-to-earth—sometimes literally. Among his best-sellers is *Underground*, which examines the world of phone lines, sewers, and subways beneath a city street. His most widely read book is *The Way Things Work*, an illustrated guide to machines and other inventions from aircraft wings to zippers.

Macaulay originally trained as an architect, and his technical background is apparent in the precision and clarity of his drawings. "I like to think of myself as an explainer first and foremost and an entertainer second," he says. Some of the things he has explained, both inside and out, can be found in the titles of his books: *Cathedral*, *City*, *Pyramid*, and *Mill*.

Don Bousquet's books have only one purpose: to make people laugh at themselves. Born in Pawtucket and raised in South County, he is Rhode Island's favorite cartoonist—and his subject is Rhode Islanders. They are, as he draws them, a scruffy, big-nosed breed who walk around with quahog rakes and fishing outfits. Instead of calling for water, his Rhode Islander lost in the desert wanders around saying, "Chowda . . . Chowda . . ." Bousquet's Rhode Islanders don't put on airs, but they are convinced that Little Rhody is the most important place in the universe. In one of his cartoons, a schoolteacher shows her class a map of New England in which Rhode Island is by far the largest state.

Bousquet started cartooning as a schoolboy. "During my high school years," he says, "I drew weird pictures of classmates and teachers while trying to ignore algebra. They put them in the class of '66 yearbook, even the ones of the principal and superintendent!" That, he says, is what started his career of "making fun of

Don Bosquet has made a career out of gently mocking his fellow Rhode Islanders.

people." The accent is on the fun; he makes Rhode Islanders look slightly dim-witted but always treats them with affection. After all, he's one himself. His cartoons appear regularly in *Yankee*, a popular New England magazine, and are collected in books with titles like *I Brake for Quahogs*, *Quahogs Are a Girl's Best Friend*, and *The Quahog Walks among Us*. "Barnes and Noble says I sell more books in Rhode Island than Stephen King," Bosquet boasts. "There are no Stephen King books with 'Quahog' in the title."

RHODE ISLANDERS IN ACTION

For some people, imaginary journeys are not enough. Rhode Island has always had its share of men and women who sought action and adventure far from home, and who risked their lives fighting for causes they believed in.

One such man was naval hero Oliver Hazard Perry, who left his South Kingstown home at age twelve and ran away to sea. He worked his way up through the naval ranks, and by the War of 1812, between Britain and the United States, he was commanding a fleet in Narragansett Bay. He was ordered to Lake Erie to elimi-nate the British fleet there. Perry's ten small ships faced six much

Oliver Hazard Perry made his name defeating a better-armed British fleet during the War of 1812.

larger British ships with more men, more guns, and more experienced crews. Sailing into combat, Perry hoisted a handmade flag proclaiming DON'T GIVE UP THE SHIP. After a hard-fought battle, his fleet defeated the British, giving the United States control of Lake Erie. Perry was hailed as the war's greatest hero. He sent a message to his commander with the famous words: "We have met the enemy and they are ours."

Women, historically, did not fight in wars, but a determined woman with a love of adventure could make her mark in other ways. Providence's Annie Peck was a great mountain climber. In 1895, she became the first woman to climb the Matterhorn in

Wanting to scale "some height where no man *had previously stood," in 1908 Annie Peck became the first person to climb Peru's Mt. Huascarán.*

Switzerland. At age sixty-one, she was the first person, man or woman, to scale the perilous 21,079-foot Mount Coropuna in Peru, where she planted a flag bearing the words VOTES FOR WOMEN. Her last great feat was climbing New Hampshire's mile-high Mount Madison—at the age of eighty-two.

RHODE ISLANDERS ONSTAGE

Providence has given the world some remarkable performers. Sissieretta Jones, the daughter of a black minister who moved to Rhode Island in 1876, enthralled the members of her church with her rich soprano voice. Barred because of her race from pursuing a career in opera, she sang songs to packed houses in New York, Boston, Chicago, the West Indies, Berlin, and even the White House. At the peak of her popularity, she wore thousands of dollars worth of jewels and traveled in her own private railway car. After more than twenty years of travel, she returned to Providence to nurse her ailing mother. Her career was over; one by one she sold her jewels, and she died in poverty.

George M. Cohan was more fortunate. "Born on the Fourth of July," as one of his songs said, of Irish parents in Providence in 1878, he entertained audiences around the nation with his spirited singing and dancing. He also wrote successful plays and such patriotic tunes as "Over There," "You're a Grand Old Flag," and "Yankee Doodle Dandy," as well as the classic "Give My Regards to Broadway."

Actor Spalding Gray is from a more modern universe. He has appeared on Broadway in *Our Town* and on-screen in *The Killing*

George M. Cohan was a master entertainer. A critic once said, "His shameless flag-waving, his sentimentality, his electricity, his rhythm, his noisiness, his brash personality were the essence of show business."

Much of Spalding Gray's material is taken from his own life. Reviewer David Sterritt once wrote that he is like a "little boy who can't help spouting every single thing that happened on his summer vacation."

Fields, but he's best known for his wry, sometimes hilarious, sometimes touching one-man shows in which he recounts stories about his own life. Raised in Barrington in the 1940s and 1950s, he says, "I never thought that I could spend a summer away from the ocean because I'd grown up in Rhode Island."

6 RHODE ISLAND HIGHLIGHTS

If you're thinking of visiting Rhode Island, you're in for a treat. You won't find majestic mountains, vast prairies, or scenic vistas that take your breath away, but you'll find a friendly, comfortable state where the traveling is easy and the food—especially Italian food and seafood—is delicious. With its beautiful beaches and nature preserves, it's a fine state for those who enjoy swimming, fishing, boating, and bird-watching. And for anyone who loves charming architecture and a sense of the past, it's unbeatable; despite its tiny size, Rhode Island contains more than a fifth of the nation's official historic landmarks.

PROVIDENCE

Rhode Island has sometimes been described as a city-state because it is so dominated by Providence. The entire state can be seen as a suburb of that city; no matter where you live (except for Block Island), you can commute to work there in less than an hour. According to former Rhode Islanders Walter and Hazel Knof, when people speak of "going downtown," they mean going to Providence.

As one of America's oldest cities, Providence has had its ups and downs. A prosperous seaport in colonial days, it became a center of commerce and industry in the nineteenth century. By the middle of the twentieth century, its once-fashionable stores were

The First Baptist Meeting House soars above the Providence skyline.

closing and businesses were leaving. Today, after decades of decline, it is thriving once again.

Recent years have seen monumental changes in the city's very shape. New shopping areas are under construction and downtown now includes a new Rhode Island Convention Center and an elegant new train station. The old railroad tracks have been rerouted;

so has Providence's river, which had long been covered over by roadway. Visible once again and spanned by a dozen new bridges in a massive effort to revitalize and beautify the city, it flows in a graceful curve past the downtown business district and the state capitol. In Waterplace, a new park by the river, you can take rides in narrow boats called gondolas, or, on summer nights, enjoy shows in the amphitheater.

These changes have excited longtime residents as well as visitors. As a writer in *Rhode Island Monthly* put it: "This is a state that moves rivers, for crying out loud, if that's what it takes to make its capital city beautiful and vital again."

In other parts of town, money has been spent not on changing the old look of the city, but on preserving it. One downtown landmark that has been preserved is the Arcade, a majestic three-story building. When it was constructed in 1828, it was revolutionary— America's first indoor shopping mall. Its huge granite pillars, each weighing more than twelve tons, were hauled one by one from a quarry in Johnston, Rhode Island, by a team of fifteen oxen. Today the Arcade is owned by Johnson & Wales University, but it is still filled with shops and cafés, much as it was over 150 years ago.

Colleges have also come to the rescue of other Providence landmarks. At the foot of College Hill the Old Stone Bank, known for its ornate gold dome, has been bought by Brown University and is being converted into a museum. "Nothing around here gets wasted," says Fox Point resident Abby Sheckley. "They used to tear old buildings down, but now they're trying to save them."

Midway up College Hill, lies beautiful Benefit Street, first laid out in 1758. Visitors are treated to "A Mile of History," with more

TEN LARGEST CITIES

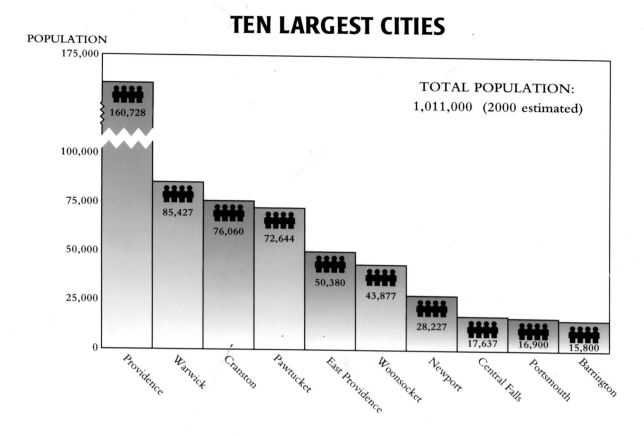

POPULATION

TOTAL POPULATION:
1,011,000   (2000 estimated)

City	Population
Providence	160,728
Warwick	85,427
Cranston	76,060
Pawtucket	72,644
East Providence	50,380
Woonsocket	43,877
Newport	28,227
Central Falls	17,637
Portsmouth	16,900
Barrington	15,800

colonial and early-nineteenth-century houses than you'll find on any other street in America. The modern electric streetlights that once lined its sidewalks have been replaced by old-fashioned flickering gas lamps. Each June, a selection of old homes in Providence—including those in the Benefit Street area—are open to the public during the Festival of Historic Houses, which never fails to attract large crowds.

One Benefit Street house that's always open to the public is the John Brown mansion, an impressive brick building dating back

PLACES TO SEE

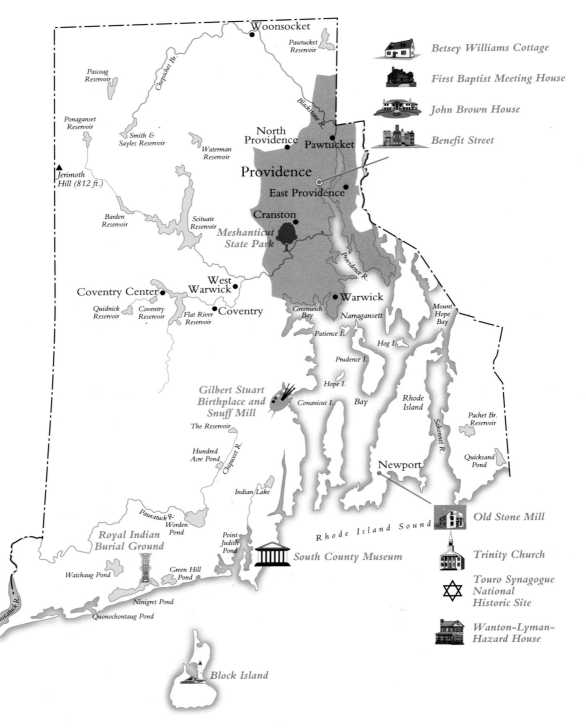

Betsey Williams Cottage

First Baptist Meeting House

John Brown House

Benefit Street

Woonsocket

Pawtucket Reservoir

Pascoag Reservoir

Chepachet Br.

Blackstone R.

Ponaganset Reservoir

Smith & Sayles Reservoir

North Providence

Pawtucket

Waterman Reservoir

Providence

Jerimoth Hill (812 ft.)

East Providence

Barden Reservoir

Scituate Reservoir

Cranston

Meshanticut State Park

Providence R.

West Warwick

Coventry Center

Coventry

Warwick

Quidnick Reservoir

Coventry Reservoir

Flat River Reservoir

Greenwich Bay

Narragansett

Mount Hope Bay

Patience I.

Hog I.

Prudence I.

Gilbert Stuart Birthplace and Snuff Mill

Hope I.

Conanicut I.

Bay

Rhode Island

Sakonnet R.

Pachet Br. Reservoir

The Reservoir

Quicksand Pond

Hundred Acre Pond

Chipuxet R.

Newport

Indian Lake

Pawcatuck R.

Worden Pond

Royal Indian Burial Ground

Point Judith Pond

Rhode Island Sound

Old Stone Mill

South County Museum

Trinity Church

Watchaug Pond

Green Hill Pond

Pawcatuck R.

Ninigret Pond

Touro Synagogue National Historic Site

Quonochontaug Pond

Wanton-Lyman-Hazard House

Block Island

to 1776. Inside are rooms furnished just as they were in the eighteenth century and decorated with reproductions of original wallpaper. On display are fine china plates and bowls that are literally *from* China, brought back in John Brown's ships, which were the first from Rhode Island to trade with that country. There's also a collection of antique dolls.

John Brown was the wealthiest member of the famous Brown family. He and his brothers Joseph, Nicholas, and Moses were Providence's most important citizens in the late 1700s. It was Joseph who designed John's house, and he must have done a good job, because President John Quincy Adams praised it as one of the "most beautiful and elegant mansions that I have ever seen on this continent." Joseph Brown also served as architect for America's oldest Baptist church, built in 1775. Crowned by a graceful 185-foot spire, the church stands just off Benefit Street six blocks from the Brown mansion.

Brown University, named for Nicholas, and the neighboring Rhode Island School of Design, a leading art school, dominate this area of Providence. Founded in 1764, Brown is America's seventh-oldest college and attracts top students from around the world. Brown's oldest building, University Hall, is a handsome red-brick structure crowned by a bell tower. According to newspaper columnist Anne Allinson, it is a building "whose architecture transmits the dignity and grace of colonial days."

Also on College Hill is peaceful Prospect Terrace, where a fourteen-foot statue of Roger Williams stands overlooking the city he founded, his right hand raised in blessing. Beneath the statue is buried what is left of Williams's body—now a handful of dust.

A statue of Roger Williams overlooks the city that he founded.

NEWPORT

Newport is Rhode Island's seventh-largest city, but as America's First Resort, it has come to stand for entertainment, sports, high society, beaches, and, in a word, fun.

Mention Newport to music lovers and they will likely think of its world-renowned folk, jazz, and classical music festivals. Dozens

PRESERVING THE PAST

Visitors to Rhode Island will find a wealth of eighteenth- and nineteenth-century houses that no other state can match—"a collection of beautiful architecture so vast," says writer Nathaniel Reade, "it's like a three-dimensional architectural textbook."

Things weren't always this way. By the late 1940s, many old homes—including some on Providence's Benefit Street—were so shabby and run-down that they were slated to be demolished. Many were to be replaced by a highway.

Concerned about the state of their city, a group of prominent citizens founded the Providence Preservation Society in 1956, and architectural historian Antoinette Downing educated Rhode Islanders about the rich architectural heritage they were about to lose. She convinced the state to sell abandoned homes cheaply to young people capable of renovating them, and she raised money to help their repair work.

In Newport, multimillionaire heiress Doris Duke formed the Newport Restoration Foundation to restore that town's colonial houses, and Katherine Urquhart Warren founded the Preservation Society of Newport County, convincing wealthy members of the community to support the maintenance of Newport's fabulous mansions. "Money is no object at all," she once said. "I could raise $100,000 or $200,000 over the lunch table any day of the week."

Thanks to these dedicated people, the past is still alive in Rhode Island.

of the most famous names in music have played there, from internationally acclaimed pianists to Louis Armstrong, Bob Dylan, Suzanne Vega, and the Indigo Girls. "A mellow crowd lazed on their chaises and quilts," one happy concertgoer recalls, "reading the Sunday paper, drinking lemonade, eating ice cream. I never saw the sun so bright, the skies so blue, the sails in Newport harbor so white. And during lulls, we could hear the waves crashing on the shore."

Mention Newport to architecture lovers and they'll think of the more than five hundred colonial-era houses still found there—more

Newport's famous Cliff Walk takes visitors past the backyards of many of the city's opulent "cottages."

than in any other city in America. But Newport is even better known as the place where the rich built their summer homes, enormous and opulent mansions that the owners jokingly referred to as "cottages." Wealthy southern landowners first began summering in Newport in the eighteenth century. The first of the celebrated cottages was Kingscote, built for a Georgia plantation owner in 1839. Today it is a museum, its elaborately decorated rooms, stained-glass windows, and expensive furnishings open to the public.

An even grander mansion is Belcourt Castle, a sixty-room home built for just one man, a thirty-five-year-old bachelor named Oliver Hazard Perry Belmont. Three hundred craftsmen were brought over from Europe to work on it. The banquet hall can seat 250 for dinner and 500 for concerts. Highlights of a visit are a reproduction of an ornate royal Portuguese coronation coach and a grand ballroom with stained-glass windows.

Some of these lavish estates border Rhode Island Sound and can be seen if you take the Cliff Walk, a three-mile-long footpath that winds along the rocky coast between the backyards of these mansions and the sea.

Those who love beautiful landscaping more than beautiful houses will enjoy an unusual nineteenth-century garden in nearby Portsmouth. Green Animals, as it's called, is a topiary garden, in which shrubs and trees are carefully clipped into familiar shapes. There are eighty such sculptures here, including twenty-one of animals. There are also greenhouses, flower beds, and a Victorian toy collection.

Newport is also called the Yachting Capital of the World. Since 1930 the waters off Newport have been the U.S. site of the America's

No city is more closely associated with yachting than Newport.

Cup race, an international competition that is the World Series of sailing. In Newport, you can take lessons in everything from sailing and windsurfing to boat repair and kayaking, or set sail on a guided cruise around the Aquidneck coast. You can also visit a replica of the *Providence*, a ship that fought in the Revolutionary War.

As you might expect, Newport has several lighthouses to help ships navigate safely. Especially well known is the one at Lime Rock, which is no longer active. In the 1800s the lighthouse keeper's daughter, Ida Lewis, became known as "the greatest saltwater heroine in American history" because she saved as many as twenty-five people from drowning—the first when she was just seventeen years old—often rowing out alone onto stormy seas with a rescue line to save boaters. The citizens of Newport rewarded her bravery with a new rowboat called the *Rescue*; it was made of mahogany and had gold-plated oarlocks and red velvet cushions.

BLOCK ISLAND

Vacationers in the 1890s called Block Island the Bermuda of the North. Today, though there are a lot more tourists and summer homes, it's still a special place of windswept dunes, low hills covered with beach grass, and views of the ocean from one's bedroom. "Block Island has the most sensational countryside of all of Rhode Island's islands," says writer Pamela Petro. "It's also the most crowded."

There isn't a lot to do on Block Island but relax, read, fish, or go for bike rides. Visitors seem to like it that way; many of them come back summer after summer. There's one other pastime for visitors: searching for pirate gold. America's first naval battle took place off the island in 1690 when a pirate named Thomas Paine, with two boats, fired on a small fleet of vessels commanded by a French pirate, Captain Picard. It's believed that one of the most infamous pirates of all, Captain William Kidd, may have buried treasure here.

Block Island is the perfect place to relax.

SOUTH COUNTY AND BEYOND

Except for the trip to Block Island, traveling in the Ocean State is not much of a chore. The state is so small that drives are not tiring, and the Newport, Jamestown-Verrazzano, and Mt. Hope Bridges—three of New England's longest bridges—span Narragansett Bay, connecting its largest islands to the mainland.

Still, some Rhode Islanders are happiest staying close to home. In one of Don Bousquet's cartoons, a backwoodsman with an ax finds himself face to face with a little space alien holding a ray-gun. "You want to abduct *me*??" the Rhode Islander says with amazement. "Listen, pal, I'm from South County and I never even go as far as Providence!"

South County is what Rhode Islanders call Washington County, the state's southern portion west of Narragansett Bay, and it's true that you can have a fine time without leaving the area, especially in the summer. Beaches such as East Matunuck, Misquamicut, Scarborough, and Narragansett attract thousands of visitors. Nature preserves such as Ninigret and Trustom Pond, with their mixture of open spaces and trees, attract migrating birds such as gulls, terns, sandpipers and ducks, and songbirds such as warblers, robins, catbirds, and flickers—as well as scores of dedicated bird-watchers.

One of the most charming spots in the county is Watch Hill at the southwestern tip of the state, a little seaside town with a few old hotels and handsome, often grand summer homes. It also has a beautiful beach, a harbor filled with pleasure boats, a single street of old-fashioned shops and restaurants, and one of America's oldest carousels, built in 1867, with hand-carved wooden horses.

Bristol, on the eastern side of Narragansett Bay, is noted for its lavish Fourth of July parade, one of the nation's largest, which also claims to be the oldest. In August comes another celebration, the two-day Quahog Festival in North Kingstown, on the western shore of the bay, where seafood of all sorts, but most notably Rhode Island's favorite clam, is downed by hungry visitors. North Kingstown's special pride is the prosperous harbor village of Wickford, which is filled with well-maintained houses from centuries past. Says one contented resident, "It is a place where time seems to have stopped in the 1820s." In short, it's like the state of Rhode Island itself—a place where the charm and beauty of the past is honored and preserved.

Newport Bridge, one of the longest bridges in New England, arches elegantly above Narragansett Bay.

Bird-watchers flock to Rhode Island's ponds in hopes of sighting rare species.

THE FLAG: The flag's white background symbolizes soldiers who lost their lives during the Revolutionary War. A gold anchor in the center of the flag represents hope and is surrounded by 13 gold stars for the thirteen original colonies. Under the anchor is a blue ribbon on which is inscribed the word "Hope," the state motto, in gold letters. The flag was adopted in 1897.

THE SEAL: A gold anchor similar to the one on the state flag appears in the center of the seal. The word "Hope" is inscribed above the anchor. At the bottom of the border that surrounds the inner part of the seal is "1636," the year Roger Williams established Providence, Rhode Island's first permanent European settlement. The state seal was adopted in 1896.

STATE SURVEY

Statehood: May 29, 1790

Origin of Name: Dutch explorer Adriaen Block called it *roodt eylandt*, meaning "red island," because of its red clay.

Nickname: Ocean State

Capital: Providence

Motto: Hope

Bird: Rhode Island Red chicken

Flower: Violet

Tree: Red maple

Stone: Cumberlandite

Mineral: Bowenite

Violet

Red maple

RHODE ISLAND'S IT FOR ME

Charlie Hall, who wrote the lyrics, created a comedy cabaret in 1992 called *Ocean State Follies*, which poked good-natured fun at Rhode Island celebrities and politicians. When challenged to write a positive song about the state he came up with a set of lyrics inspired by the state's natural beauty. Maria Day, a cast member of the follies, wrote the melody. The song was adopted officially in 1996.

Lyrics by Charlie Hall

Music by Maria Day

GEOGRAPHY

Highest Point: 812 feet, at Jerimoth Hill

Lowest Point: Sea level, along the Atlantic coast

Area: 1,214 square miles

Greatest Distance, North to South: 48 miles

Greatest Distance, East to West: 37 miles

Bordering States: Connecticut on the west, Massachusetts to the north and east

Hottest Recorded Temperature: 104°F at Providence on August 2, 1975

Coldest Recorded Temperature: -23°F at Kingston on January 11, 1942

Average Annual Precipitation: 44 inches

Major Rivers: Blackstone, Moshassuck, Pawcatuck, Pawtucket, Providence, Seekonk

Major Lakes: Ninigret Pond, Point Judith Pond, Quonochontaug Pond, Watchaug Pond

Trees: ash, beech, birch, cedar, dogwood, elm, hemlock, hickory, maple, oak, pine, poplar, willow

Wild Plants: aster, buttercup, cattail, daisy, fern, goldenrod, lily, scarlet pimpernel, rhododendron, seaweed, trillium, violet, wild carrot, wild rose

Animals: beaver, fox, hare, mink, mole, muskrat, opossum, otter, rabbit, raccoon, squirrel, white-tailed deer, woodchuck

Birds: barred owl, blue jay, catbird, crow, duck, eagle, flicker, hawk, osprey, partridge, pigeon, sparrow, tern

Fish: bluefin tuna, bluefish, cod, eel, flounder, mackerel, perch, pike, sea bass, shark, striped bass, swordfish, trout

Shellfish: blue crab, lobster, mussel, oyster, quahog, scallop, soft-shell clam

Endangered Animals: American burying beetle, Atlantic leatherback turtle, Atlantic sea turtle, peregrine falcon, roseate tern

American burying beetle

Endangered Plants: adder's-tongue, foxtail club moss, purple Cliffbrake, New England boneset, northern blazing star, slender arrowhead, stiff club moss

Northern blazing star

TIMELINE

Rhode Island History

c. 1400 Narragansett and Wampanoag Indians live in present-day Rhode Island

1524 Italian navigator Giovanni da Verrazano explores Narragansett Bay

1614 Dutch navigator Adriaen Block lands on what is later named Block Island

1636 Roger Williams establishes Providence

1638 William Coddington, John Clarke, Anne Hutchinson, and others found Portsmouth

1639 Roger Williams and Ezekiel Holliman found America's first Baptist church, the Baptist Society of America, in Providence

1644 Roger Williams obtains a charter from England for the Rhode Island colony

1663 King Charles II grants Rhode Island a second charter, which provides for religious freedom and self-governance

1699 Quakers in Newport set up colony's first Quaker meetinghouse

1739 Spaniards seize smuggler Robert Jenkins's ship and cut off his ear, thus beginning the War of Jenkins's Ear, or King George's War

1764 Rhode Island College, which later becomes Brown University, is founded

1776 Two months before signing the Declaration of Independence, Rhode Island becomes first colony to renounce allegiance to England

1790 Rhode Island becomes the 13th state

1835 Rhode Island's first railroad begins operation between Providence and Boston

1842 Thomas Dorr leads reform movement known as Dorr's Rebellion, which demands voting rights for all adult white males

1882 Public schools become mandatory

1883 U.S. Navy opens Newport Naval Station

1900 Providence becomes Rhode Island's sole capital

1938 A severe hurricane results in 317 deaths and $100 million in property damage

1954 First U.S. jazz festival held in Newport

1969 Rhode Island's sector of Interstate 95 is completed

1969 Newport Bridge over Narragansett Bay opens

1971 State personal income tax is approved

1973 U.S. Navy shuts down Quonset Point Naval Air Station

1990 Rhode Island celebrates 200th anniversary of statehood

1991 Crandall family of Westerly, unable to afford the taxes on their 350-acre farm valued at over $1 million, relinquishes the farm to the Narragansett Indians after 532 years of ownership

ECONOMY

Agricultural Products: apples, dairy products, hay, potatoes, poultry, snap beans, squash, sweet corn

Manufactured Products: appliances, boats and ships, electrical equipment, farm machinery, jewelry, metal products, printed materials, rubber products, silverware

Apple picking

Natural Resources: coal, granite, graphite, iron, limestone, sandstone

Business and Trade: communications, finance, insurance, real estate, retail trade, transportation, wholesale trade

CALENDAR OF CELEBRATIONS

Polar Bear Plunge The hearty welcome New Year's Day the hard way, when members of the Newport Polar Bear Club, who swim outdoors year-round, are joined by amateurs and spectators as they dare to enter the icy water and revel in the new year.

Newport Winter Festival This festival offers a break from the dreariness of winter for ten days in late January and early February. You can see fireworks, attend concerts and dogsled races, enter a snow-sculpting contest, and take a carriage ride through the wintry streets of the city.

Rhode Island Spring Flower and Garden Show Spring blooms early at the Rhode Island Convention Center in Newport. Each year a specific type of garden is featured.

Convergence—Annual Festival of the Arts This summer-long event is sponsored by the Providence Parks Department and features visual and performing arts, dance, music, and theater. A favorite among visitors are the sculptures displayed in Roger Williams Park and in downtown Providence. The festival features music to satisfy every taste—you can hear everything from chamber music to an Afro-Cuban band.

Apponaug Village Festival Each June visitors can enjoy a flea market and craft show that brings out the best talent in Warwick. There's also pony rides and plenty of food.

Children's Day Kids get a chance to experience games of the past during this June celebration in Bristol. At the Cogeshall Farm Museum youngsters can play popular games of the 18th century, including ninepins, sticks and loops, and top spinning. It's a great day to enjoy some old-fashioned fun.

Children's Day

Summer Pops and Fireworks Music is in the air during the last part of June at the Wilcox Park grounds in Westerly. Past acts included the Chorus of Westerly and the Boston Festival Orchestra.

Newport Folk Festival Every August since 1958 Newport has hosted the very best in established and up-and-coming artists. Performers who have taken the stage include Bob Dylan, Joan Baez, James Taylor, Richard Thompson, and the Indigo Girls.

JVC Jazz Festival The second weekend in August brings the sound of jazz to Newport. For over 40 years, the best in traditional and modern jazz have shared their music and energy with Newport residents and visitors alike.

Harvest Fair In early October, a country fair in Middletown makes autumn a delight for visitors. Among the featured events are hayrides, sack races, a rope walk, and a greased pole climb—a challenge for everyone. Listen to local performers while sampling the baked goods and enjoying the crafts on display.

Harvest by the Sea Festival During October, Newport County residents enjoy apple cider and pumpkin-carving contests while participating in the autumn whale watches. There's plenty to see and do as the crisp air awakens everyone's appetite, which can be satisfied at the farmers' market.

Montgolfier Day Balloon Regatta Hot-air balloons lend festivity and color to the Providence sky in late November. The balloons are launched from the statehouse lawn to the thrill of spectators. The regatta commemorates the first manned balloon flight in Paris in 1783.

Christmas at Blithewold From Thanksgiving to Christmas, the Blithewold

Mansion and Gardens in Bristol are aglow with the traditional finery of the holidays. You can see an 18-foot tree, glowing wreaths, and an amazing spectacle of flowering plants and greenery.

Festival of Lights Celebrate an old-fashioned Christmas in Kingstown with hayrides, storytelling, and caroling, and tour the beautiful homes of North Kingstown during the month of December.

STATE STARS

William Alison (Bill) Anders (1933–   ) was a crew member of *Apollo 8*, which in 1968 became the first manned space-craft to circle the moon. Anders was a longtime resident of Providence.

William Alison Anders

Leonard Bacon (1887–1954) was a poet who made his home in Peace Dale. He won the 1941 Pulitzer Prize in poetry for his collection *Sunderland Capture and Other Poems*.

Joseph Brown (1733–1785) was a renowned architect born in Providence. His First Baptist Meeting House, located in Providence, is considered among the finest examples of colonial architecture.

Moses Brown (1738–1836) launched the cotton manufacturing industry in America when, in Pawtucket, he built the first textile mill to use water-power to manufacture cotton thread. He also led the effort to abolish slavery in Rhode Island. Brown was born in Providence.

Nicholas Brown (1729–1791) directed the family businesses, which included slave trading, distilling rum, and producing iron products. Brown was instrumental in convincing state leaders to ratify the U.S. Constitution. Because he was influential in establishing Rhode Island College and provided much support to the college, it was renamed Brown University in his honor.

Nicholas Brown

George M. Cohan (1878–1942) is considered the father of musical comedy in America. A composer, producer, actor, songwriter, and playwright, he set musicals in America rather than in foreign lands. He won the Congressional Medal of Honor for his patriotic World War I song "Over There." Cohan was born in Providence.

Thomas Wilson Dorr (1805–1854) led an uprising that became known as Dorr's Rebellion. Dorr and his followers created a new state constitution, known as the People's Constitution, which gave voting rights to all white adult males.

Jabez Gorham (1792–1869) was the father of Rhode Island's silverware industry. Born in Providence, he founded Gorham Manufacturing Company, which became the world's largest producer of sterling silver.

John Milton Hay (1838–1905) served as private secretary to President Abraham Lincoln. As U.S. secretary of state from 1889 to 1905, he helped formulate American's Open Door policy toward China. Hay graduated from Brown University, which later named a library in his honor.

Julia Ward Howe (1819–1910) was a reformer, writer, and poet who lived in Portsmouth and Newport. Best known for writing the words to "The Battle Hymn of the Republic," she also published travel sketches and social criticism. Howe actively worked for the abolition of slavery.

Julia Ward Howe

Anne Hutchinson (c. 1600–1643) was a religious enthusiast and one of the founders of Rhode Island. Born in England, she immigrated to Boston in 1634. Her religious views caused problems for her and she was excommunicated from the Boston church and settled with her followers in Rhode Island.

Christopher Grant La Farge (1862–1938) was an architect who specialized in designing churches. Born in Newport, he ran the firm that designed the interior of St. Paul the Apostle Church in New York City.

Jacob Lawrence (1907–   ) is a painter who often portrays historical events and social issues that have affected African Americans. His paintings show busy street scenes, pool halls, and men and women working. Although born in New Jersey, he lived a great deal of his life in Rhode Island. He is known as the patriarch of today's black painters.

Jacob Lawrence

Ida Lewis (1842–1911) was the lighthouse keeper on Lime Rock in Newport Harbor for fifty years. Born in Newport, she was the daughter of a sea captain. During her career, she performed many rescues, beginning in 1859 when she saved four men whose boat had capsized. Susan B. Anthony reported Lewis's exploits in her suffrage journal the *Revolution*. Lewis was awarded a gold medal by Congress and a pension by the Carnegie Hero Fund.

H. P. Lovecraft (1890–1937) was an important writer of horror and supernatural fiction. Born in Providence, he lived there most of his life. He wrote his first story, "Dagon," in 1917, which was eventually published in *Weird Tales* magazine. Many of Lovecraft's stories were published in this magazine. His stories and novels are set in recognizable New England settings, which sometimes seem realistic and other times seem dreamlike.

David Macaulay (1946–   ) is a celebrated writer. Macaulay studied architecture at the Rhode Island School of Design, but his interests led him to write and illustrate books that inform his readers of the world around them. His books include *Cathedral*, *City*, and *Pyramid*. In 1988, he published *The Way Things Work*, a book that teaches how everyday things do what they're intended to do. In 1991, his book *Black and White* won the Caldecott Award for the year's best picture book. His entertaining, informative books appeal to both children and adults. Macaulay taught at the Rhode Island School of Design for ten years.

Horace Mann (1796–1859) is known as the father of American public education. He graduated as valedictorian from Brown University in 1819 and then began a distinguished career in education, leading the movement to make education accessible to every child. He also served as the first head of the Massachusetts state board of education.

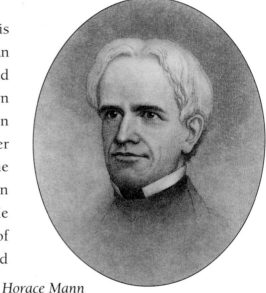

Horace Mann

Annie Smith Peck (1850–1935) was a feminist, mountaineer, and Greek scholar. Born in Providence, she became the first woman to attend the American School of Classical Studies in Athens. Later she taught Latin at Smith College. Peck began climbing the Alps at age 45 and was a founding member of the American Alpine Club in 1902. She climbed and traveled well into her eighties.

Oliver Hazard Perry (1785–1819) commanded ships in the Great Lakes during the War of 1812. His famous words, "We have met the enemy and they are ours," were issued after his heroic victory on Lake Erie. He was born in South Kingstown.

Samuel Slater (1768–1835) built America's first water-powered cotton-spinning machine in Pawtucket. Slater manufactured the machine based on his memory of machinery invented by Englishman Richard Arkwright. Thus began the American cotton industry.

Samuel Slater

Gilbert Stuart (1755–1828) painted portraits of noted people of his time, such as the first five presidents of the United States. He is best known for his portraits of George Washington, including the one that appears on the one-dollar bill. He was born in North Kingstown.

Chris Van Allsburg (1949–   ) is a writer and illustrator of children's books. Born in Michigan, he received a master's degree from the Rhode Island School of Design in 1975. He has taught illustration there since 1977. Van Allsburg has won Caldecott Medals for his illustrations for *Jumanji* and *The Polar Express*. In 1993, he won the Regina Medal, in honor of his lifetime contribution to children's literature.

Roger Williams (1603?–1683) is regarded as the founder of Rhode Island. He advocated religious tolerance and democracy and wrote about his principles of religious freedom in *The Bloudy Tenent of Persecution*.

He maintained friendly relations with the Indians of the region after founding Providence in 1636. Williams served as president of Rhode Island colony after it was chartered in 1644.

Leonard Woodcock (1911–   ), an American labor leader and diplomat, was born in Providence. He became vice president of the United Automobile Works (UAW) in 1955 and was elected president of the UAW in 1970. In 1979, President Jimmy Carter named him U.S. ambassador to China.

TOUR THE STATE

Benefit Street (Providence) This Mile of History is an impressive array of colonial homes. Walking through this hilly district, you can see many eighteenth- and nineteenth-century houses.

Roger Williams Park Zoo (Providence) The more than 900 animals at the zoo live in exhibits that recreate the African plains, the American tropics, and other regions. Children can also enjoy a special birthday party at the zoo.

Roger Williams National Memorial (Providence) Built on the site of the original Providence settlement of 1636, this memorial features displays commemorating Williams's contribution to democracy and religious freedom, including an audiovisual presentation describing Williams's life.

Roger Williams Park Museum of Natural History (Providence) This museum contains an abundance of artifacts to delight visitors, including tools that whalers brought back from the South Pacific. The planetarium makes this museum doubly worth a stop.

The Arcade (Providence) This magnificent structure houses the nation's oldest shopping mall. Built in 1828, this marketplace still thrives and features international boutiques and eateries.

Statehouse (Providence) Modeled after the U.S. Capitol in Washington, D.C., this structure boasts the second-largest self-supporting marble dome in the world. A statue of the Independent Man stands atop the dome to symbolize Rhode Island's history of religious freedom. Visitors can also view Gilbert Stuart's full-length portrait of George Washington.

Slater Mill Historic Site (Pawtucket) At this site, craft exhibits and working machinery tell the tale of the birth of the American industrial revolution. Among the exhibits is the nation's first water-driven cotton mill.

Green Animals Topiary Gardens (Portsmouth) Have you ever seen a shrub that reminded you of a giraffe? At this garden, you will see a giraffelike bush, along with 80 other sculptured trees and shrubs that look like camels, peacocks, wild boars, and other creatures. Next to these gardens is a museum featuring children's toys and furniture from the 19th century.

Green Animals Topiary Gardens

Norman Bird Sanctuary (Middletown) You can enjoy the breathtaking beauty of Rhode Island at this 450-acre area of ridges, valleys, and ponds. The sanctuary is devoted to the protection of native plants and animals and the preservation of unique landforms.

Newport Historical Society (Newport) Here visitors can view displays of documents and artifacts from the area's colonial days.

Hammersmith Farm (Newport) The only working farm in Newport, Hammersmith Farm is best known as the "summer White House" of President John F. Kennedy. Built in 1887, the 28-room cottage was the site of Kennedy's wedding reception.

The Breakers (Newport) Visit the mansion where steamship and railroad tycoon Cornelius Vanderbilt lived. Built in 1895, this spectacular 70-room mansion was modeled after Italian villas.

Adventureland (Narragansett) How would you like to visit an island, venture deep into a cave, and then drive a go-cart? You can do all this and more at this park, which also features an 18-hole miniature golf course and many lovely waterfalls.

Museum of Primitive Art and Culture (Narragansett) Here you can view art and artifacts made by American Indians as well as people from the South Seas and Africa.

Tomaquag Indian Memorial Museum (Exeter) This museum displays a large collection of local and regional Indian artifacts.

Great Swamp Fight Monument (South Kingstown) This stone obelisk memorializes the Narragansett and Wampanoag Indians who were massacred during King Philip's War in 1675. The nearby Great Swamp

Management Area has walking trails where visitors may see many varieties of wildlife, including mink, raccoons, deer, and owls.

South County Museum (South Kingstown) This museum contains over 10,000 items from early Rhode Island life—everything from a country kitchen to a maritime display. Walk the nature trails and visit a historic cemetery before heading off to the many demonstrations and lectures that help you understand the life and times of Rhode Island long ago.

Quonset Aviation Museum (North Kingstown) If you like aircraft, a visit here is a real treat. Many military aircraft are on display, including a Russian MIG-17. You can also see aircraft in different phases of restoration as the staff works on upcoming exhibits.

The Enchanted Forest of Rhode Island (Hopkinton) A children's favorite, this amusement park features theme rides geared at children. After riding the Ferris wheel and roller coaster, you can play a game of miniature golf and then head over to the batting cages. A petting zoo adds to the fun.

Block Island A popular family vacation spot, this island features beautiful beaches, hiking trails, wildlife sanctuaries, and the Southeast Lighthouse.

FUN FACTS

Rhode Island was the first free republic of the New World. The Rhode Island general assembly formally declared the colony's independence from Great Britain on May 4, 1776. The other twelve colonies joined the cause exactly two months later.

The oldest synagogue in the United States is located in Newport. The Touro Synagogue was completed in 1763 and is still standing today.

Newport holds a special place in transportation history. America's first traffic law was enacted there in 1678, when the authorities banned galloping horses on local streets. In 1904, it was also the site of the nation's first speeding ticket, which was given to a motorist who insisted on driving more than 20 miles per hour. (He was fined $15 for his first offense, and jailed for doing it again.)

The Pawtucket Red Sox, a minor league team, played in the longest game in baseball history. It ran 32 innings on April 18, 1981, before being stopped. When it was resumed two months later, the PawSox won in the 33rd inning, beating Rochester, 3–2.

FIND OUT MORE

If you would like to learn more about the Ocean State, look in your local library or bookstore or on the Internet. Here are a few titles to get you started:

GENERAL STATE BOOKS

Fradin, Dennis B. *Rhode Island*. Danbury, CT: Children's Press, 1995.

Thompson, Kathleen. *Rhode Island*. Chatham, NJ: Raintree Steck-Vaughn, 1996.

Warner, J. F. *Rhode Island*. Minneapolis: Lerner, 1993.

SPECIAL INTEREST BOOKS

Avi. *Finding Providence: The Story of Roger Williams*. New York: Harper-Collins, 1997.

Bousquet, Don. *I Brake for Quahogs*. Wakefield, RI: Recreation Publications/Narragansett Graphics, 1984.

Drake, Samuel Adams. *A Book of New England Legends and Folklore*. Rutland, VT: Charles E. Tuttle, 1971.

FICTION

Avi. *Something Upstairs: A Tale of Ghosts*. New York: Orchard Books, 1988. Supernatural tale with a Rhode Island setting.

DeFelice, Cynthia. *The Apprenticeship of Lucas Whittaker*. New York: Farrar, Strauss, and Giroux, 1996. A 12-year-old Rhode Island boy becomes a doctor's apprentice in 1849 after his parents die.

Flood, E. L. *Secret in the Moonlight*. Mahwah, NJ: Troll, 1994. A girl living on a small island in Narragansett Bay becomes involved in a search for pirate treasure after the arrival of two sinister adult treasure hunters.

Jordan, Sandra. *Christmas Tree Farm*. New York: Orchard Books, 1993. Describes life on a Rhode Island tree farm through the four seasons.

INTERNET SITES

www.brainiac.com/ri/narragansett
Information on the Narragansett Indian tribe's history and present activities.

www.projo.com
The *Providence Journal-Bulletin* website, with local news, commentary, and a live one-frame-per-minute camera view of various locations in downtown Providence.

www.cs.brown.edu/fun/pps/home.html
This Providence Preservation Society site provides detailed walking tours, with maps and photos, of Benefit Street and downtown Providence.

www.visitrhodeisland.com

All sorts of tourism information and trip-planning material, courtesy of the Rhode Island Economic Development Corporation.

www.sec.state.ri.us

The secretary of state's office provides information on current legislation, recent elections, state officials, government agencies, and Rhode Island history, plus a directory of Rhode Island businesses, a tour of the capitol, and links to Rhode Island towns.

INDEX

Page numbers for charts, graphs, and illustrations, are in boldface.